JEFFERSON BETHKE

BIBLE STUDY WRITTEN WITH JEREMY MAXFIELD

IT'S NOT WHAT YOU THINK

WHY CHRISTIANITY IS ABOUT SO MUCH MORE
THAN GOING TO HEAVEN WHEN YOU DIE

LifeWay Press®
Nashville, Tennessee

Published by LifeWay Press® • © 2015 Jefferson Bethke

ISBN 978-1-4300-3196-3 • Item 005644107

Dewey decimal classification: 248.84
Subject headings: ETERNAL LIFE \ CHRISTIAN LIFE \ IMMORTALITY

To order additional copies of this resource, write to LifeWay Resources Customer Service; One LifeWay Plaza; Nashville, TN 37234-0113; fax 615.251.5933; phone toll free 800.458.2772; email orderentry@lifeway.com; order online at www.lifeway.com; or visit the LifeWay Christian Store serving you.

Printed in the United States of America

Groups Ministry Publishing • LifeWay Resources
One LifeWay Plaza • Nashville, TN 37234-0152

CONTENTS

ABOUT JEFFERSON

Jefferson currently lives on Maui with his wife, Alyssa, and daughter, Kinsley.

He has authored *Jesus > Religion* and *It's Not What You Think.*

Besides writing, Jefferson makes YouTube videos, which have been seen collectively 62 million times, and hosts a podcast with his wife that can be found on iTunes.

His passion is to see people follow Jesus and come to a true, life-giving understanding of the free grace of God for us all.

Jefferson also has a yellow lab named Aslan and enjoys reading good books and drinking good coffee in his downtime.

Jefferson's contact information is below. Feel free to share your story, ask a question, or just say hello. Use *#INWYTbook* to share any thoughts with the world.

Twitter	*www.twitter.com/jeffersonbethke*
Instagram	*www.instagram.com/jeffersonbethke*
Pinterest	*www.pinterest.com/jeffersonbethke*
Facebook	*www.facebook.com/jeffersonbethkepage*
YouTube	*www.youtube.com/bball1989*
Blog	*www.jeffbethke.com*

INTRODUCTION

Recently, in my own study and journey with Jesus and the Scriptures, I started to realize there are certain things about the first-century world that make Jesus and the Scriptures more vibrant, beautiful, and compelling. When you understand His world, you begin to understand Him. There are things that make no sense to us because we don't know what it was like to be a first-century rabbi or a Jew living in Judea under Roman rule.

But when we enter into the world of Jesus, and take Him for who He was, the Bible begins to turn to color. Details we haven't noticed before jump out at us. Neither the Bible nor Jesus changes; but stepping back into the first century gives us new eyes to see who He was, what He did, and why we are still talking about Him today.

I hope through these pages you might begin to see Jesus more vibrantly yourself. I'm not a pastor or theologian, and I don't have numerous degrees where people need to call me Doctor or Professor Bethke. But over the past couple of years I've fallen more in love with Jesus and the story of God and His church by unclicking the mute button twenty-first-century Westerners have put on first-century Jesus and letting Him speak on His own.

Every morning as I walk with Jesus, I ask Him to open our eyes more and more each day. Because when we see Jesus clearly, then we can follow Him.

One of the scariest questions we have to ask ourselves is, what if we aren't seeing Jesus properly? What implication does that have for our lives? What if Jesus isn't who we think? I believe He's always catching us off guard, creatively challenging us, pursuing us, and loving us.[1]

---

1. From Jefferson Bethke, *It's Not What You Think: Why Christianity Is About So Much More than Going to Heaven When You Die* (Nashville: Thomas Nelson, 2015).

HOW TO USE THIS STUDY

It's Not What You Think is a six-session Bible study. Most groups meet weekly, completing one session a week, but feel free to follow a plan that meets the needs and schedule of the people in your group.

Each session of *It's Not What You Think* consists of two major sections of content, each with its own distinct features: group and personal.

1. Each session opens with group content, including:

START

This page includes questions to get the conversation started and to introduce the video segment.

WATCH

This page includes Scripture references from Jefferson's teaching and space to take personal notes while watching the video.

RESPOND

This page includes questions and statements to help you and your group respond to the Bible and Jefferson's video teaching.

Everyone will be able to participate and benefit from the group content simply by showing up for each session. Think of this time together as a great starting point. Group discussion is an important step in personal growth.

Tips for leading a group can be found on the following pages (pp. 8–9). Leaders are provided with valuable help to make sure everyone's time studying *It's Not What You Think* is a life-changing experience.

MORE FROM THE BOOK

The end of each group session provides a suggestion for how group members can go even deeper into the topics covered in the video by reading related chapters in *It's Not What You Think: Why Christianity Is About So Much More than Going to Heaven When You Die* by Jefferson Bethke (Thomas Nelson, 2015, ISBN 978-1-4002-0541-7).

2. Each session offers individual content, including:

PERSONAL READING & REFLECTION

Each session of this Bible study includes three mini-studies to complete on your own.

These pages are designed to help you discover what God's Word has to say about the topic you've discussed in your group session. They include selected Bible verses and questions to help you understand or apply what you're reading. This content guides you to a deeper understanding of the biblical truths presented and discussed in the group time.

The goal of this section isn't to fulfill a religious obligation and check Bible reading off your spiritual to-do list. The goal of this personal study is to help you grow in your relationship with Jesus.

Personal relationships naturally include spending time with people, getting to know them, and listening to what they say. This is true with Jesus too. The more time you spend in God's Word, the better you get to know Him.

These pages are also designed to help you creatively process what you're studying. You'll be prompted to interact with drawings and to record your own thoughts, feelings, and prayers.

Remember, the suggested study plan isn't a rigid formula; it's all about helping you grow in your personal relationship with Jesus.

TIPS FOR LEADING A GROUP

PRAYERFULLY PREPARE

Prepare for each session by—
reviewing the weekly material and group questions ahead of time;
praying for each person in the group.

Ask the Holy Spirit to work through you and the group discussion as you point to Jesus each week through God's Word.

MINIMIZE DISTRACTIONS

Create a comfortable environment. If group members are uncomfortable, they'll be distracted and therefore not engaged in the group experience. Plan ahead by taking into consideration—
seating;
temperature;
lighting;
food or drink;
surrounding noise;
general cleanliness (put pets away if meeting in a home).

At best, thoughtfulness and hospitality show guests and group members they're welcome and valued in whatever environment you choose to gather. At worst, people may never notice your effort, but they're also not distracted. Do everything in your ability to help people focus on what's most important: connecting with God, with the Bible, and with others.

INCLUDE OTHERS

Your goal is to foster a community in which people are welcome just as they are but encouraged to grow spiritually. Always be aware of opportunities to—
invite new people to join your group;
include any people who visit the group.

An inexpensive way to make first-time guests feel welcome or to invite people to get involved is to give them their own copies of this Bible study book.

ENCOURAGE DISCUSSION

A good small group has the following characteristics.

Everyone participates. Encourage everyone to ask questions, share responses, or read aloud.

No one dominates—not even the leader. Be sure what you say takes up less than half of your time together as a group. Politely redirect discussion if anyone dominates.

Nobody is rushed through questions. Don't feel that a moment of silence is a bad thing. People often need time to think about their responses to questions they've just heard or to gain courage to share what God is stirring in their hearts.

Input is affirmed and followed up. Make sure you point out something true or helpful in a response. Don't just move on. Build personal connections with follow-up questions, asking how other people have experienced similar things or how a truth has shaped their understanding of God and the Scripture you're studying. People are less likely to speak up if they fear that you don't actually want to hear their answers or that you're looking for only a certain answer.

God and His Word are central. Opinions and experiences can be helpful, but God has given us the truth. Trust Scripture to be the authority and God's Spirit to work in people's lives. You can't change anyone, but God can. Continually point people to the Word and to active steps of faith.

KEEP CONNECTING

Think of ways to connect with group members during the week. Participation during the group session is always improved when members spend time connecting with one another away from the session. The more people are comfortable with and involved in one another's lives, the more they'll look forward to being together. When people move beyond being friendly and in the same group to truly being friends who form a community, they come to each session eager to engage instead of merely attending.

Encourage group members with thoughts, commitments, or questions from the session by connecting through—

emails;

texts;

social media.

When possible, build deeper friendships by planning or spontaneously inviting group members to join you outside your regularly scheduled group time for—

meals;

fun activities;

projects around your home, church, or community.

SESSION ONE

STORY

START

Welcome everyone to session 1.
Begin with the following questions and comments.

What's your favorite story of all time? It can be a book, a movie, a show, a play, or any other medium.

Why is this your favorite story?

In your opinion, what makes a great story?

Over the next six sessions we're going to look at major themes throughout the pages of Scripture. We'll begin today by focusing on the way we view the Bible and how that perspective shapes our understanding of everything else in life. Keep the following question in mind as we begin this Bible study and watch the first video.

How does the way I view the Bible affect my life?

WATCH

Use the space below to take notes or sketch ideas as you watch the video for session 1.

SCRIPTURES: Ephesians 6:17; Hebrews 4:12; Genesis 1; Genesis 3:24; Genesis 12:1-3; Exodus 19:6; Isaiah 53; Matthew 4:19

Video sessions available at
www.lifeway.com/NotWhatYouThink

RESPOND

Use these statements and questions to guide a group discussion.

Jefferson shared some limited views of the Bible (sword and road map for life). How would you describe the ways you've viewed Scripture?

How does viewing the Bible as a story affect the way you read Scripture? The way you see God? The way you see yourself?

Jefferson said, "You matter, but you're not the center of the story." What does that mean? What negative consequences result when we see ourselves at the center of Scripture's story?

Jefferson mentioned the theme in Genesis of people moving east and west. Are you currently (1) moving east, away from God's authority; (2) moving west, seeking God's presence; or (3) moving back and forth, wrestling with what you want?

Would you say you're running, drifting, limping, or wandering toward or away from God? Why did you describe your spiritual walk this way?

Read Matthew 4:19.

In what ways is Christianity not just about going to heaven when you die but also about following Jesus into a bigger story now?

Jesus called men who were ordinary and even overlooked by the religious leaders of their day. How does that fact encourage you?

What else in the video was helpful, encouraging, or challenging for you? Why?

Wrap up with prayer. Encourage everyone to complete the personal reading & reflection on the following pages before your next group session.

MORE FROM THE BOOK: To go even deeper into the topics covered in this session, read chapter 1 in *It's Not What You Think: Why Christianity Is About So Much More than Going to Heaven When You Die* by Jefferson Bethke (Thomas Nelson, 2015).

PERSONAL READING & REFLECTION
1. YOUR STARTING POINT

Imagine that you're looking at the still surface of glassy water. Maybe it's somewhere familiar, like a puddle gathered against the curb after a hard rain. Or maybe it's an ideal setting, like your favorite spot on the lake for watching a sunset. Maybe you're staring into your dog's bowl half-asleep as you sip your coffee. It can be anything.

Get a clear picture in your mind and describe it below. (Trust me.)

Now imagine something in your hand. It could be any shape or size. Picture the scene as the object falls, drips, or is thrown into the water. As something breaks into the still water and disturbs any reflections across the surface, what happens? What sound is made? How does the water move and for how long?

Describe what you see in your mind.

No matter how big or small something is, no matter how loud or quiet the splash is, when something hits the surface of the water, ripples are made. Right? Did you see the ripples? These concentric circles get bigger and bigger, reaching farther and farther, going on forever until an opposing force like friction, gravity, or a boundary stops them.

According to NASA (who first put a man on the moon, so they know a few things about movement and gravity), "Newton's first law states that every object will remain at rest or in uniform motion in a straight line unless compelled to change its state by the action of an external force. This is normally taken as the definition of *inertia.*"[1]

OK. Great. So what's the point of this little mental exercise and science lesson?

What if I told you that your view of the Bible has a ripple effect? It's the starting point from which everything else we're going to look at flows. The way you see the Bible affects the way you see God, the way you see yourself. Really, the way you respond keeps rippling into the way you see everything else in life (and beyond).

So let's be sure to get a clear picture of what the Bible is. In the video during the group session, we looked at a simple grid that showed this ripple effect. Look at some of the examples below of how this chain reaction can play out.

BIBLE	GOD	YOU
Sword	Captain	Warrior
Road map	Direction giver	Traveler
Promise book	Gift giver	Gift getter
Rule book	Judge	Game player
Law	King	Citizen
Story	Author	Part of story

In your own words explain the way you see the Bible.
Use as many words as needed in the space below.

Now try summarizing what you just wrote in a single word or phrase. Write it in the first space below.

BIBLE	GOD	YOU

If that's how you see the Bible, what does that make God,
according to that perspective? Write a word or phrase in
the second space above.

Finally, if that's how you see the Bible and God, what does that
make you, according to that perspective? Write that word or
phrase in the third space above.

15

What do you think of the ripple effect flowing from your starting point? Had you ever thought through this before? Do you like what this reveals about God and your life?

Write your thoughts in the space below.

Honestly, do you enjoy reading the Bible?

Yes   No   Sometimes

When and where do you most enjoy reading the Bible?

Why is that a good time and place for reading the Bible?

Why do you read your Bible? If you don't read it often (or ever), why not? (Don't worry. This isn't a legalistic checklist. This is just to help you think about things.)

All the ideas in the chart on page 15 have at least some truth to them. The Bible is multifaceted, like a diamond. There are many angles from which we can see parts of it, but ultimately, it's one big, beautiful story. These other perspectives are subnarratives, or smaller parts of the big story, the metanarrative.

To see the Bible for what it is, we need the right starting point. What better starting point than looking at what the Bible says about itself? Let's see how all the parts fit together to give us a full picture of how to read and respond to the Bible.

Read 2 Timothy 3:16-17.

How do these verses describe the Bible?

What do these verses say about the usefulness of Scripture and the way we're to respond to it?

The phrase "inspired by God" (v. 16) or "God-breathed" (NIV) describes the power and nature of Scripture as God's Word. The Bible isn't just words about God. The Bible is God's Word to us. We'll look more at the power of God's Word in the next section of this week's study, but for now let that amazing reality sink in: God is speaking to you through the Bible. He's telling you something. He's letting you know who He is and who you are. He's telling you the great story that's been unfolding since before time began and will continue into eternity.

Take a minute to record your thoughts or a prayer reflecting on the awesome truth that God can speak to you today and every day through His Word—the Bible.

1. "Newton's Laws of Motion," *National Aeronautics and Space Administration* [online], 5 May 2015 [cited 19 August 2015]. Available from the Internet: *www.grc.nasa.gov/www/K-12/airplane/newton.html.*

2. THE POWER OF GOD'S WORD

In the beginning God …
GENESIS 1:1

These are the very first words in the first sentence on the first page of the first book of the Bible. By the way, the Bible is one big story, but it's made up of 66 books. Think of it like a series. Right away we can see that this story is (and always has been) about God.

Read Genesis 1:1–2:3.

Notice the phrase repeated at the beginnings of Genesis 1:3,6,9,14,20,24,26. How did God create everything?

Several repeated phrases in this opening scene give us incredible insight into the main character of the story. (If you like to highlight, underline, or circle things in your Bible, this is a helpful way to notice patterns or understand and remember what you're reading.)

Record the number of times you see the following words in Genesis 1:1–2:3 (or similar words, depending on your translation).

"God":

"Said":

"It was so":

"It was good":

"Blessed":

What does the repetition of these words reveal about God and His Word?

It's pretty amazing to think about the formless and empty darkness becoming everything we experience through our senses today. It all came into being in response to God's voice. Darkness was filled with light. Emptiness was filled with life.

C. S. Lewis described a scene like this in *The Magician's Nephew,* the first book in his classic series *The Chronicles of Narnia.* In that fictional creation account Aslan the lion is the king and creator of the world known as Narnia. He creates everything by singing over the space, and the tone of his voice sends forth ripples of life as everything bubbles up and springs into existence in the wake of his song.

The point of Genesis is less about exactly how physical matter works and more about the good, powerful, and wise Creator—God. Everything is under His authority. His power is absolute. His word has authority. His design is good.

Do you remember what you read in the previous section? Second Timothy 3:16 says:

All Scripture is God-breathed.
NIV

All Scripture is breathed out by God.
ESV

All Scripture is inspired by God.
HCSB

All Scripture—the Bible—is God's Word. It's powerful, authoritative, life-giving, and good.

Even Jesus quoted the following Scripture from the the Old Testament when He was hungry and was tempted to use His miraculously creative power to make food for Himself during a season of intense prayer and fasting:

It is written, "Man must not live on bread alone but on every word that comes from the mouth of God."
MATTHEW 4:4

To get the full power of this statement (or any verse in the Bible), we need to consider the context. These words are profound in and of themselves, but keep in mind that Jesus had been tempted to turn stones into bread after not eating anything for 40 days! When Jesus quoted Deuteronomy 8:3, He essentially said He can give up physical needs for a long period of time but couldn't give up trust in and obedience to God's Word for even a moment.

How would you describe your need for God's Word?

Jesus demonstrated that the Word of God is powerful in guarding our lives from spiritual attack and in fighting temptation. The Bible describes God's Word as our sword (see Eph. 6:17). Again, it's important to keep context in mind. This image for God's Word comes in the context of spiritual warfare; it's not a weapon to be used against other people (see Eph. 6:12).

One other time the Bible compares itself to a sword is in the Book of Hebrews:

> The word of God is living and effective and sharper than any double-edged sword, penetrating as far as the separation of soul and spirit, joints and marrow. It is able to judge the ideas and thoughts of the heart. No creature is hidden from Him, but all things are naked and exposed to the eyes of Him to whom we must give an account.
>
> **HEBREWS 4:12-13**

Here the image highlights personal accountability. The razor-sharp nature of the sword is like a scalpel, revealing what's inside our hearts. Again, the purpose is spiritual, but in this case, it's God wielding the sword, not us. It's a picture of God's absolute authority, power, wisdom, and justice.

How has reading and knowing Scripture helped you when facing temptation?

When has Scripture convicted you of sin in your heart?

It's important to understand that God's Word isn't just functional but a source of joy. If you have time, read all of Psalm 119. You'll be overwhelmed with the infinite goodness of God's Word. The whole chapter is an acrostic poem (meaning each new section begins with the next letter of the Hebrew alphabet, the original language in which it was written), and the subject is the value of and joy of Scripture. Look at some of the creative ways the psalmist described his delight in God's Word:

How happy are those whose way is blameless,
who live according to the LORD's instruction!
PSALM 119:1

I have treasured Your word in my heart
so that I may not sin against You.
PSALM 119:11

How sweet Your word is to my taste—
sweeter than honey in my mouth.
I gain understanding from Your precepts;
therefore I hate every false way.
PSALM 119:103-104

Your word is a lamp for my feet
and a light on my path.
PSALM 119:105

I long for Your salvation, LORD,
and Your instruction is my delight.
Let me live, and I will praise You;
may Your judgments help me.
I wander like a lost sheep;
seek Your servant,
for I do not forget Your commands.
PSALM 119:174-176

Circle, underline, or highlight positive words in the previous verses that describe the nature of God's Word or feelings about it.

Notice that the first verse mentions happiness when we trust and obey God's Word but that the last admits the need for God to save and help us since we're naturally prone to wander like lost sheep. This is the great tension in the story of Scripture.

End your study time by thanking God for His Word. If you'd like, create a poem or an acrostic describing God's Word.

3. A BIGGER AND BETTER STORY

There's a video on YouTube of some people who set up 10,000 iPhones like dominoes and then tipped them over in this insane progression that was perfectly timed to travel all over an office building. Besides being crazy expensive—Where do you even get that many iPhones?—it took some serious planning and execution. Maybe you've tried setting up domino patterns before. What makes them both so amazing and so frustrating is that one little bump sets the whole thing off, whether or not you mean to do it.

In the first section of your study this week, you saw the domino effect (or the ripple effect) with your view of the Bible. The way you see the Bible affects the way you see God, which then affects the way you see yourself. They all flow into one another. Once one idea starts leaning in one direction, everything else follows.

The trajectory of your life will continue in its current direction unless something stops you and changes your direction. The story of the Bible shows a pattern of people falling away from God and the way He interrupted our downward spiral of self-destruction.

In the second section of study, you saw that in the beginning God created everything in heaven and on earth by the power of His Word. He spoke it all into existence. Nothingness obeyed Him and become something. God looked at everything, blessed it, and said it was good. Everything was in perfect balance, harmony, and rhythm. But then something happened. The order of the universe tipped and made a mess of everything.

Genesis 3 tells the familiar story of Adam and Eve in the garden of Eden. Life on earth was never better, but the man and the woman God created chose to disobey Him. You might think the original sin was eating the forbidden fruit. That's partly true; that was the visible action that broke the one and only rule God stipulated. God had established a healthy boundary in His goodness, and the man, the woman, and all creation were flourishing.

The problem began the instant they entertained the idea that God shouldn't be trusted and that He wasn't really good. They wondered whether there was a bigger and better story than the one God was telling them. They gave in to the temptation of seeking happiness apart from God and the way He designed life to work. Despite this epic tragedy, one that would send shockwaves throughout history by introducing sin into the world, we see glimmers of hope.

Read Genesis 3.

Describe Adam and Eve's immediate response to their sin (see vv. 7-8).

Describe God's immediate response (see v. 9).

What do God's presence and question reveal about Him?

From that point we see human relationships break as Adam and Eve started passing the blame, nobody owning up to their responsibility for the defiant act. Consequences and curses shattered the entire created order. Sin had fractured everything to its core.

But in His goodness God came to and called out for the man and the woman, sacrificially provided clothing to cover their shame, and mercifully guarded them from the tree of life so that they wouldn't be separated forever from a personal relationship with Him (see vv. 9,21-24).

Underline, circle, or highlight the direction mentioned in each of the following verses as human history began unraveling.

He drove man out and stationed the cherubim and the flaming, whirling sword east of the garden of Eden to guard the way to the tree of life.
GENESIS 3:24

Cain went out from the LORD's presence and lived in the land of Nod, east of Eden.
GENESIS 4:16

After Adam and Eve's sin, they were banished to the east. After their son, Cain, sinned, he was banished east. From that point Genesis describes the growing brokenness of humanity, with the sole exception of a faithful family line from Adam through another

NOT WHAT YOU THINK

son, Seth, to Noah, to Abram, who would become Abraham (see Gen. 4–12). Abram, in contrast to this general trend, moved from Ur (near the Persian Gulf) to Canaan (near the Mediterranean Sea) and even temporarily into Egypt—a general pattern of moving west.

I don't need to overspiritualize and exaggerate the action of literally moving in any direction, but the symbolic pattern in the story of Genesis sets up a major theme in Scripture: running from God or following Him in faith.

According to this pattern in Genesis, are you currently—
1. **moving away from God's authority?**
2. **moving closer toward God's presence?**
3. **moving back and forth, wrestling with what you want?**

How would you describe your movement in relation to God?

Running   Limping   Wandering   Other:

Why did you describe your spiritual journey this way?

God invited Abraham to join the story He'd been telling since the beginning, one of mercy and love and blessing. Unlike Adam, who hid in shame when God called, Abraham responded in faith, following God even when He didn't understand where He was going.

Read Hebrews 11:1-19.

What word is repeated over and over as the obvious theme in that summary of biblical history?

Record Hebrews 11:1 in the space below.

How would you describe the importance of faith, according to verses 2 and 6?

Abraham trusted what God said. He lived on earth as a citizen of heaven. Living on earth as a citizen of heaven is a major theme throughout the story of Scripture, and it's a major focus for this Bible study. Abraham's story of living by faith, even in relation to his son Isaac, ultimately pointed to Jesus. Every story told in Hebrews 11 (and in the entire Bible) points to Jesus.

When Jesus called His disciples, they too were ordinary people who had to trust that He was truly inviting them into a bigger and better story than the one they were living. That's what faith is—acting on your belief in God. It's responding to His invitation to join Him in a bigger and better story.

Read Matthew 4:18-22.

How do stories of ordinary people who lived by faith encourage you? Are there other people in history or in your life who inspire you to trust God's Word and live by faith? If so, who?

If someone looked at your life to write your biography or make a documentary film, what would your life story be about?

If your story is about anything other than following God's call— if anything else is at the center of your life—what needs to change so that your life points to Jesus?

A tension exists in a life of faith. You matter, but you're not the center of the story. Your life isn't about you. This is actually an incredibly freeing reality. Unlike Adam and Eve, who fell for the lie that there was a better story than the one God had given them, everyone who lives by faith and follows Jesus enters the story God has been telling since day one. In His own words Jesus told those He'd called to follow Him exactly why He came:

I have come so that they may have life and have it in abundance.
JOHN 10:10

TEMPLE

START

Welcome everyone. Start by reviewing session 1 before introducing session 2.

Session 1 focused on the domino effect our view of Scripture has on our views of God and ourselves.

What was most helpful, encouraging, or challenging from your personal reading and reflection in session 1?

Today we'll focus on the themes of pursuit and relationship in the big story of Scripture.

Who in the group has gone to great lengths to achieve something or to be with someone? Briefly share stories.

Why would someone be willing to pursue something or someone, even at great personal cost?

We love stories of pursuit and relationship. Keep the following question in mind as we watch the next video.

If the story in the Bible about a relationship with God is true, how will you respond?

WATCH

Use the space below to take notes or sketch ideas as you watch the video for session 2.

SCRIPTURES: Genesis 1:27; Exodus 29:45-46; Exodus 32:8-9; John 1:1; John 1:14; Acts 2:1-4; 1 Corinthians 3:16; Revelation 21:22; Habakkuk 2:14; Psalm 47:8; Hebrews 12:2

RESPOND

Use these statements and questions to guide a group discussion.

What comes to mind when you hear the word *temple?*

How does the reality that the whole earth is filled with God's presence affect the way you see your daily life?

Read Genesis 1:27.

How does being created in the image of God affect your view of God? Of yourself? Of the way you interact with others?

Read 1 Corinthians 3:16.

If you're a Christian, how does having the Spirit inside you change the way you live?

How does seeing God as pursuing you change your view of Him? Why does it require a response from you?

Jefferson asked how you'd respond to God's pursuit of a relationship with you through Jesus. How have you responded to His call?

What else in the video was helpful, encouraging, or challenging for you? Why?

Wrap up with prayer. Encourage everyone to complete the personal reading and reflection on the following pages before your next group session.

MORE FROM THE BOOK: To go even deeper into the topics covered in this session, read chapters 2 and 6 in *It's Not What You Think: Why Christianity Is About So Much More than Going to Heaven When You Die* by Jefferson Bethke (Thomas Nelson, 2015).

PERSONAL READING & REFLECTION
1. MADE IN HIS IMAGE

Let's start with a quick review of what we've covered so far before diving into what's next. In the previous session you saw these three major points:

1. Your starting point is going to have a ripple effect, influencing the overall direction of your life. More specifically, the way you approach the Bible is going to shape your views of God and of yourself.

2. The Bible is God's Word. God created everything by the power of His command. As the Creator, He has absolute authority and knows what's best for our happiness.

3. Human history has been a constant pattern of turning away from God's loving authority and seeking happiness apart from Him. But the Bible tells the story of how God calls broken people back to abundant life through faith in Jesus.

Hopefully you're starting to see that Christianity is about so much more than going to heaven when you die. Just as people in the Bible walked with God and followed Jesus by faith, your life today matters. It's not because you have to take advantage of every second to earn enough points to win a spot in heaven. Living by faith doesn't mean we ignore this world and try to climb up to heaven. In fact, the Bible reveals that the opposite is true.

This week we'll look more at three more major points:

1. People are unique among all God's creation.

2. God didn't take any shortcuts in making Himself known and in making a relationship with Him possible.

3. Life radically changes when you understand that God doesn't live off in a distant corner of outer space called heaven. He also isn't limited to sacred buildings or places.

When you read the creation story in session 1, you may have noticed another pattern that we didn't focus on previously.

What do the following verses say were created "according to their kinds" or "according to its kind" in Genesis 1?

Verse 11:

Verse 12:

Verse 21:

Verse 24:

Verse 25:

But God broke His pattern in the story, drawing added emphasis to the unique nature of this particular part of His good creation:

> God said, "Let Us make man in Our image, according to Our likeness. They will rule the fish of the sea, the birds of the sky, the livestock, all the earth, and the creatures that crawl on the earth."
>
> So God created man in His own image;
> He created him in the image of God;
> He created them male and female.
> **GENESIS 1:26-27**

Underline every time the words *image* and *likeness* are used in Genesis 1:26-27.

Circle every reference to God (including *God, Us, Our, His, He,* and *own)* in Genesis 1:26-27.

Draw a box around every reference to humans (including *man, him, them, male,* and *female)* in Genesis 1:26-27.

How does being created in the image of God encourage you personally? How is it convicting?

In what ways do you see people turning away from what God's Word says about human beings, both male and female, being created uniquely in the image and likeness of God?

If you trust God's Word, believing that people are created in His image, how does it change the way you see and relate to God?

We'll go even deeper into these things later, but it's important to start thinking about them now. The Bible has layer after beautiful layer of amazing truth, especially when it comes to our relationship with God. You'll see when we circle back to certain ideas how the ripple effect is at work, constantly growing and building on our understanding of Scripture. For now let's focus on this idea of being made in the image of God and the way it relates to two simple ideas introduced in session 1: faith and sin.

Imagine yourself as a mirror that's positioned to perfectly reflect light at a right angle. Above the vertical line, write the word *Creator*. Beside the horizontal line write the words *created things*. Inside this triangle write the word *faith*.

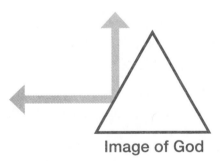

Image of God

This simple picture illustrates God's perfectly good design for you. Another word for this goodness according to God's design is *righteousness*. When you're living by faith, you're in right relationship with God and with everything and everyone in His creation. This is where you experience the true happiness mentioned in Psalm 119:1.

Now imagine yourself as a mirror that's turned away, facing created things instead of your Creator. Inside this triangle write *sin*.

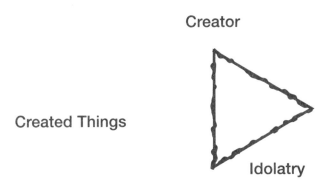

Creator

Created Things

Idolatry

Sin twists and distorts the likeness of God in us, like a mirror in a fun house at a carnival. We haven't lost the image of God, but it's broken. As long as we remain in this condition, we can never relate properly to God or to anyone or anything He created, no matter what we try. (Go ahead. Try drawing different lines to reflect off this second image. It's hopeless.)

Read Romans 1:22-23.

What things have you turned to for happiness instead of God?

Anything you turn to instead of God is an idol. It's easy to dismiss verses that mention idols, because you probably don't pray to physical images of a deity, but putting yourself or anything else God created as the focal point of your life is sin. It's idolatry.

You were made in the image of God. He designed you to reflect His goodness, His righteousness, and His glorious likeness into the world around you.

Pray now that God will help you turn your focus to Him in faith. Ask forgiveness for any idolatry in your heart and thank Him for the goodness He's revealed to you through His Word.

2. GOD WITH US

See, the virgin will become pregnant and give birth to a son, and they will name Him Immanuel, which is translated "God is with us."

MATTHEW 1:23

Shocking. Scandalous. Unthinkable.

These probably aren't words you associate with Christmastime. But each year on December 25, we celebrate one of the most unexpected and pivotal moments in all of history. An unwed, teenage virgin gave birth to God in the flesh. God not only became a human but was also born a poor little baby. It's a key part of the story God has been telling since the beginning of time. The story—and even our Bibles—started well before the birth of Baby Jesus and continues long after He was crucified, buried, and resurrected in glory.

It was and still is unusual, to say the least, to believe in a Deity who's all-powerful, all-knowing, and ever-present yet also vulnerable—pursuing us, serving us, and even dying for us.

Religion is about what people must do to get up to the gods and maybe into some kind of heaven. Christianity is about what God has done, is still doing, and will do to come down and be with us, bringing heaven with Him.

It's easy to take for granted the extraordinary nature of the story of God as revealed in Scripture. Let's trace the steps God took to continually humble Himself, coming down to be among His people.

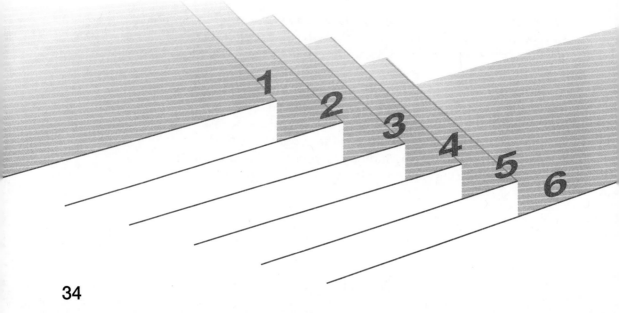

Genesis begins by using language similar to that of building a temple. In the creation story you see God creating three environments on days 1–3, filling those environments on days 4–6, placing His image in His creation, and then declaring a holy time of rest and celebration on day 7. The heavens and the earth were like God's original temple.

DAY 1	DAY 2	DAY 3
Light & dark	Sea & sky	Land & vegetation
DAY 4	**DAY 5**	**DAY 6**
Sun, moon, & stars	Fish, sea creatures, & birds	Land creatures & human beings

DAY 7
Holy day of rest and blessing

From the very beginning God intended to dwell among His people. We even saw in the story of creation and the fall into sin that God was in the habit of walking around in the garden and talking to Adam and Eve in a personal way (see Gen. 3:8-9.)

On the top step (STEP 1 on p. 34) write "Heaven and earth."

How does it shape the way you view life to think God created the world—both time and space—as a holy place to be with us?

The very first thing the Bible tells us is that God is the Creator of everything. But He's not a distant Creator. He wants to be with us and has never stopped pursuing us. Even after humankind fell into sin, rebelling against God in the garden, He continually called people into a relationship with Him. We saw earlier that He called Abraham. God then blessed the family line of Abraham, connecting back to Adam and forward to what would become the nation of Israel. He would save the nation through Moses and begin dwelling among His people again in a visible way, then through King David and his son, Solomon, and eventually through Jesus—Immanuel.

Read Exodus 29:45-46; 40:34-38.

On STEP 2 (p. 34) write "The tabernacle."

Why is it significant that God had a visible presence among the entire community of people as they followed Him? What does that reveal about God? How would it benefit people?

Read 1 Kings 8:10-20; 9:1-9.

On **STEP 3** (p. 34) write "The temple."

Why is it significant that God had a consistent presence among His people? What does that reveal about God? How would it benefit people?

Read John 1:1-5,14.

On **STEP 4** (p. 34) write "Jesus."

Why is it significant that God became a man—that the Creator was not only in His creation but also part of it? What does that reveal about God? How would it benefit people?

Read Acts 2:1-4,17-23,37-40.

On **STEP 5** (p. 34) write "The Holy Spirit."

Why is it significant that God began giving His Spirit to all people who turned away from sin and lived by faith? What does that reveal about God? How would it benefit people?

Read Revelation 21:1-5,22-27.

On **STEP 6** (p. 34) write "New heaven and earth."

Why is it significant that in the future God will again have a visible presence among His people? What does this reveal about God? How does it excite you and give you hope?

If you really want to be blown away, read the following chapters to see how much God cares about every detail in the way He relates to us: creation, Genesis 1–2; tabernacle, Exodus 25–31; 35–40; temple, 1 Kings 5–9; future, Revelation 21–22.

It's overwhelming to realize how much God wants to dwell with us. In the final passage you read describing our future, you see a bride being presented to a groom. Our loving Father provides for His family and wants everything to be perfect in celebration of the joy and love between Christ and His people, the church.

In Acts 2:37-40 Peter said everyone has to decide whether they'll put their faith in Jesus. To those who do, God then gives His Spirit. Everyone who has the Spirit will live forever in the joyful presence of God the Father, Jesus the Son, and all His people.

Take a few minutes to reflect on the amazing reality that over the course of human history, God has been pursuing a relationship with His people. Realize that He's specifically pursued a personal relationship with you. Express your response below.

Now describe the moment you realized God was pursuing you and the way you responded to Him through faith in Jesus. When did it happen? What got your attention? What changed in your thoughts, feelings, and actions? Whom did God use to introduce you to Jesus, and with whom did you share your good news?

3. A LIVING TEMPLE

The tabernacle and the temple were visible, tangible places of worship and evidence of God's presence among His people. God provided detailed directions about those who could interact with the sacred spaces and how they were to do so. These beautifully ornate places were sources of great joy and hope for God's people. And they would cause the whole world to recognize the Israelites as a community identified by faith in God.

But when Jesus entered the story as God in the flesh, everything changed. The temple and the religious practices surrounding it had become a source of arrogant pride and division. Jesus took everyone's understanding of the temple and turned it upside down when He declared:

> Destroy this sanctuary, and I will raise it up in three days.
> **JOHN 2:19**

Read John 2:13-22.

What new meaning did Jesus introduce to sanctuary or temple?

What evidence did Jesus give for His passion against human-centered religion and for a God-centered life?

How are you sometimes distracted by meaningless (and possibly even divisive), self-centered religion?

What would it look like for Jesus to chase out selfish religion in your heart? What would He get rid of and overturn?

While Jesus was physically walking the earth, He was the sacred place where heaven and earth met. He was the intersection of the holy and the human. He was 100 percent God and 100 percent man. He was the true temple. As revolutionary as this fact was, He made an even more radical (and, at the time, even more confusing) promise.

Read John 14:1-12.

Just as God designated a very specific way to approach Him in the tabernacle and the temple, what did Jesus say is the only way to enter a personal, eternal relationship with God?

A lot of people want to argue that this it's narrow-minded to believe in only one God and one way to experience life with Him forever. But what Jesus said here is that God, our Heavenly Father, was throwing the door to the house wide open. While it used to be that only certain people could enter the temple at certain times in certain ways, now anybody who believes in Jesus can enter God's presence. And not only can we enter His presence, but He is also now closer than anybody had ever imagined.

What did Jesus promise His followers?

When have you felt that believing in and following God would be easier if you could see and hear Him? Why would that be better?

That's pretty amazing by itself, but Jesus went on to promise even more.

> If you love Me, you will keep My commands. And I will ask the Father, and He will give you another Counselor to be with you forever. He is the Spirit of truth. The world is unable to receive Him because it doesn't see Him or know Him. But you do know Him, because He remains with you and will be in you. I will not leave you as orphans; I am coming to you.
> **JOHN 14:15-18**

I am telling you the truth. It is for your benefit that I go away, because
if I don't go away the Counselor will not come to you. If I go, I
will send Him to you. When He comes, He will convict the world
about sin, righteousness, and judgment: About sin, because
they do not believe in Me; about righteousness, because I am
going to the Father and you will no longer see Me; and about
judgment, because the ruler of this world has been judged.

I still have many things to tell you, but you can't bear them now.
When the Spirit of truth comes, He will guide you into all the truth.
For He will not speak on His own, but He will speak whatever He
hears. He will also declare to you what is to come. He will glorify
Me, because He will take from what is Mine and declare it to you.

JOHN 16:7-14

**Why did Jesus say it's actually for our benefit that He isn't
with us in a physical body anymore?**

Jesus told His followers they'd be able to do even more than He did while He was with
them because they'd be empowered by the same Spirit. Even basic math tells us that
millions of Christians can have a greater presence than one Jesus. You may be thinking,
But I'm not Jesus! True. But Jesus said we all have the same Spirit. That's pretty amazing.

Let this truth sink in. Jesus said it's for your good and for His glory that He gives you the
Spirit instead of His physical presence on earth. That means you're now His temple:

Don't you yourselves know that you are God's
sanctuary and that the Spirit of God lives in you?

1 CORINTHIANS 3:16

Have you ever thought of yourself as a temple?   Yes   No

**How does it change the way you view your life to know that
the Spirit of God—the same Spirit Jesus had—lives in you?**

How does it change the way you view other believers to know they're temples with God's Spirit dwelling in them?

How does it change what you desire for nonbelievers to realize that although they have a broken image of God in them, they don't have His Spirit?

This isn't just symbolic language about Jesus being in your heart. The Bible says several times that the Spirit of God is literally within people who put their faith in Jesus. When God first sent the Spirit, there was clear evidence of this fact. The constant theme of the Book of Acts is the evidence and power of the Holy Spirit in the lives of Christians.

It's easy to think of the Spirit in abstract or symbolic terms, if we think about Him at all. So let's look at some very practical realities about the Holy Spirit.

The Spirit convicts you of sin and righteousness (see John 16:8), leads you into all truth (see John 16:13), empowers you to share the gospel (see Acts 1:8; 4:31), gives you hope and love (see Rom. 5:5), frees you from sin and death (see Rom. 8:2), testifies that you're God's child (see Rom. 8:16), helps you pray for what you need (see Rom. 8:26), searches the mind of God (see 1 Cor. 2:10), teaches you spiritual truth (see 1 Cor. 2:13), and gives you life (see 2 Cor. 3:6).

God has a life-changing plan for you. He's not finished telling His story of changing the world, and now He's doing it through your life. But the best part is that He's not asking you to do great things *for* Him; He's inviting you to do great things *with* Him. He's giving you everything you need. He *is* everything you need.

God's Spirit inside you is like a deep breath when you're taking a leap of faith. Life is an adventure, and you can live in—and live as—the overlap between heaven and earth. He gives you strength and power, enabling you to experience a bigger and better story.

Close by thanking God for the many ways the Spirit is at work in and through you right now.

SESSION THREE
KINGDOM

START

Welcome everyone. Start by reviewing session 2 before introducing session 3.

Session 2 focused on God's continuous pursuit of a personal relationship with His people.

What was most helpful, encouraging, or challenging from your personal reading and reflection in session 2?

Today we'll shift our attention to the disruptive nature of the gospel.

When have you caused a disturbance—intentionally or accidentally? Briefly share stories.

Nobody expected God to enter history in the person of Jesus. Today we'll see how disruptive it was for the King of the universe to enter the world He created. Keep the following question in mind as we watch the next video.

Who or what is in the position of authority over your life?

WATCH

Use the space below to take notes or sketch ideas as you watch the video for session 3.

SCRIPTURES: Luke 22:70; John 18:37; Acts 2:36-40; John 2:19; Matthew 4:17; Matthew 6:10; 1 Thessalonians 5:18; John 13:3-17; Matthew 5:39-45; Matthew 20:28; John 13:35

RESPOND

Use these statements and questions to guide a group discussion.

How are Christians known? What is their reputation?

Read John 13:34-35.

How would you describe the love of Christ?

How would it change things if Christians were known for Christlike love—even for enemies? What specifically would change in your life?

Read Matthew 5:38-47.

How does living with such radical love reveal our identities as citizens of a different kingdom and as children of our Heavenly Father? How is the love of Christ unlike the so-called love and good deeds of the world?

When have you had to love someone who was difficult to love? When has someone shown you unnatural kindness that you didn't deserve?

Jefferson concluded by asking two takeaway questions: (1) Are you letting the rule of Jesus order your priorities? (2) Are you going out as a kingdom citizen to show people the greatness of our King?

How would you answer those questions, and how will you live them out in practical ways?

What else in the video was helpful, encouraging, or challenging for you? Why?

Wrap up with prayer. Encourage everyone to complete the personal reading and reflection on the following pages before your next group session.

MORE FROM THE BOOK: To go even deeper into the topics covered in this session, read chapters 3 and 7 in *It's Not What You Think: Why Christianity Is About So Much More than Going to Heaven When You Die* by Jefferson Bethke (Thomas Nelson, 2015).

PERSONAL READING & REFLECTION
1. THE KING'S GOOD NEWS

Let's start with a quick review of what we covered in the previous session before diving into what's next. Last time we looked at three major points:

1. People, both male and female, are unique among God's creation. We're made in His image. Sin distorted the image of God, and all creation was broken as a result of sin.

2. God didn't abandon us in our sinful condition to live and die apart from Him forever. Throughout history He's constantly pursued a relationship with people He's called out to live by faith. The way He related to His people became increasingly more vulnerable and personal in nature. Eventually, we'll live in a perfectly restored heaven and earth with God.

3. Life radically changes when you understand that God doesn't live off in a distant corner of outer space called heaven. He isn't limited to sacred buildings or places either. You're the temple of His Spirit. The same Spirit that raised Jesus from the dead lives inside you and every Christian.

So now what do you do with this amazing-but-true story?

1. You start to understand what it really means to live as part of God's kingdom, not just in heaven when you die but right here and now on earth.

2. As someone who's created in the image of God and filled with His Spirit, you begin to see that the greatest need of everyone around you is to join this epic drama and life-giving reality.

3. The Holy Spirit conforms you more and more to the likeness of Jesus as you follow Him in obedience. Jesus commanded you to continue His mission of inviting other people into a right relationship with God.

Let's start exploring this idea of the kingdom by first looking at the word *gospel*.

What do you think of when you hear the word *gospel*?

Who first explained the gospel to you? How did they explain it?

Most of us, even if we do a Google search or look *gospel* up on Wikipedia, think of it as a religious message about Jesus or the books of the Bible specifically about Jesus (Matthew, Mark, Luke, and John). The other possible meaning is that *gospel* is synonymous with absolute truth. In other words, somebody might say, "Football is gospel" or "The gospel according to my coach," meaning that the only thing that matters is this topic or what this person says. Life revolves around that subject. Ironically, even this cultural usage reflects a conviction that Jesus' life story is absolutely true.

Now let's consider what people would have thought of the word *gospel* during the time of Jesus and when the New Testament was being written. Look at the opening lines in the Gospel of Mark, which, most scholars agree, was the first Gospel written, around A.D. 65 to 70:

> The beginning of the gospel of Jesus Christ, the
> Son of God. As it is written in Isaiah the prophet:
>
> Look, I am sending My messenger ahead of You,
> who will prepare Your way.
> A voice of one crying out in the wilderness:
> Prepare the way for the Lord;
> make His paths straight!
> **MARK 1:1-3**

Gospel isn't a word that was unique to Christians. *Gospel* wasn't even originally a religious word. It came from words used by rulers, in particular Caesar in the Roman Empire. The word *gospel* is from *euangelion* in Greek or *evangelion* in Latin, meaning *good news.* When good news was spread throughout the empire of a great victory or of a new caesar, it would be proclaimed by messengers *(evangelizo,* from which we get our word *evangelists)*.

This was the culture and context Jesus entered and in which the message of His life, victory over death, salvation, and kingdom was first preached, recorded, and spread throughout the world.

How does the word *evangelize* now relate to Jesus?

What comes to mind when you think of an evangelist?

Caesar Augustus, the adopted son of the deified Julius Caesar, founded the Roman Empire shortly before the birth of Jesus (see Luke 2:1). His stepson, Tiberius Caesar, was the emperor during Jesus' ministry, crucifixion, and resurrection and during the earliest days of the Christian church (see Luke 3:1). At the time the Gospel of Mark was written, Nero, the great-great-grandnephew of Augustus, was the emperor and began officially and infamously persecuting Christians, blaming them for a fire that burned much of the city of Rome—a fire many believe Nero started.

The caesars in power as the story of Jesus unfolded claimed the titles Son of the Divine, King of Kings, and Lord of Lords. Evangelists spread "good news" throughout the empire about Caesar to maintain order, establish peace, and celebrate mighty victories.

Do you see how dangerously subversive the language of the gospel story of Jesus was at the time? What has become religious vocabulary was loaded with revolutionary language. This fact helps explain what Jesus was asked by the Roman leader, how He was mocked, what was written on His cross, and what the Roman soldier said after His death:

> Pilate asked Him, "Are You the King of the Jews?"
> He answered him, "You have said it."
> **MARK 15:2**

> They dressed Him in a purple robe, twisted together
> a crown of thorns, and put it on Him. And they
> began to salute Him, "Hail, King of the Jews!"
> **MARK 15:17-18**

The inscription of the charge written against Him was:
THE KING OF THE JEWS.
MARK 15:26

When the centurion, who was standing opposite Him, saw the way
He breathed His last, he said, "This man really was God's Son!"
MARK 15:39

To follow Jesus meant declaring your allegiance to a king other than Caesar and a kingdom other than Rome. It was to declare that Jesus was the truly divine Son, King of kings, and Lord of lords. To evangelize others, spreading the good news of His victory over death from sin and the coming of His heavenly kingdom to earth, was radical, to say the least.

But the gospel of Jesus was much bigger than any earthly political empire or military victory. It was much bigger than the legalistic box in which religion had tried to keep God. Jesus was setting people free from sin and death. Look at Jesus' first words in the Gospel of Mark:

The time is fulfilled, and the kingdom of God has come near.
Repent and believe in the good news!
MARK 1:15

From what do you need to repent?

Practically, what does it look like for you in the 21st century to believe in the good news that Jesus is your King?

Let's wrap up this section of study by reflecting on this thought: If believing in the gospel were as radical in our culture today as it was two thousand years ago (and it still is in some parts of the world), what would you do?

2. AMBASSADORS OF THE KING

If you've ever wondered what your purpose is in life or what you're supposed to do as a Christian, here's some great news. You've been given a mission. Check out Jesus' final words to His disciples. (If you want the context, read the resurrection account in Matt. 28.)

> All authority has been given to Me in heaven and on earth. Go, therefore, and make disciples of all nations, baptizing them in the name of the Father and of the Son and of the Holy Spirit, teaching them to observe everything I have commanded you. And remember, I am with you always, to the end of the age.
>
> **MATTHEW 28:18-20**

Underline the first and last sentences in the previous passage. How are those words encouraging?

If you've never memorized Scripture, this is a good place to start. These words of Jesus are often referred to as the Great Commission. It wasn't intended just for Jesus' disciples standing there at that moment. When Jesus commanded them to teach others to observe everything He'd commanded them, that included this Great Commission. Your job, as part of the kingdom, is to go make other disciples. You're to teach others what you've been taught and to share your experiences.

But Jesus' disciples still didn't get it. By the way, that should be pretty encouraging if you've ever felt you're a little slow catching on to this spiritual stuff. These guys had been with Jesus for three years of teaching and miracles and had seen Him killed, buried, and resurrected for 40 days. Yet the very last thing they asked Him missed the point:

> When they had come together, they asked Him, "Lord, are You restoring the kingdom to Israel at this time?" He said to them, "It is not for you to know times or periods that the Father has set by His own authority. But you will receive power when the Holy Spirit has come on you, and you will be My witnesses in Jerusalem, in all Judea and Samaria, and to the ends of the earth."
>
> **ACTS 1:6-8**

When you realize how subversive and threatening to the status quo the gospel of Jesus and the kingdom of God originally were, hopefully an excited (and maybe a good kind of nervous) passion starts burning in you like a fire.

The gospel is still that radical. It still changes everything. We just forget it, having grown jaded from familiarity and taking it for granted since we have such easy access to God's Word. People don't always want to hear it, but they need to. You needed it, right?

One of the Old Testament prophets described knowing the truth this way:

If I say, "I won't mention Him
or speak any longer in His name,"
His message becomes a fire burning in my heart,
shut up in my bones.
I become tired of holding it in,
and I cannot prevail.
JEREMIAH 20:9

Two of Jesus' followers described it this way:

We are unable to stop speaking about what we have seen and heard.
ACTS 4:20

How would you describe your passion and enthusiasm to share the gospel of God's kingdom?

On a scale of 1 to 10, how often do you talk about Jesus?

1	2	3	4	5	6	7	8	9	10
Never									Constantly

If you don't talk about Jesus often, why not? If you do, what do you most enjoy talking about?

Read 2 Corinthians 5:17-21.

As part of God's kingdom, you've received a new identity. What is it, according to this Scripture?

To reconcile means *to make things right.* Having been reconciled to God through Jesus, we now join the work of bringing everything and everyone back under the rule of our King — not by force or manipulation (that's the way of the world) but by the power of the gospel and our witness in word and deed. We're ambassadors, continuing the same work Jesus began. This means when He says He has all authority and then sends us out, promising always to be with us by His Spirit, we now have His power and authority to act on behalf of the kingdom.

Remember, in the beginning God created heaven and earth in perfect harmony. There was *shalom,* the Hebrew word meaning *peace.* We could think of it like this:

In Genesis 3 sin broke everything. Shalom was shattered. It's common to think of earth and physical things as bad and heaven and spiritual things as good but completely separate. (That was an early heresy, by the way.) Christians often mistakenly think our job as Christians is to escape earth and get into heaven when we die:

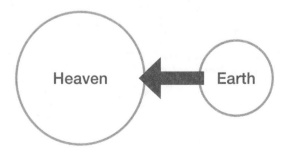

But Christianity and the gospel are so much better than that. The Bible tells us that God has constantly maintained a connection with us. There's always been a point of overlap between heaven and earth, from the garden, to the tabernacle, to the temple, to Jesus. And now it's us. It's you. More specifically, it's His Spirit in you. As a living temple of the Holy Spirit, you're now the point of overlap between heaven and earth, the physical and the spiritual.

And because you're an ambassador of reconciliation, your job is to bring little pockets of heaven with you wherever you go—home, work, school, church, the street, the beach—everywhere.

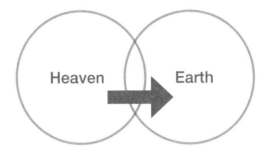

Think of as many places as you can think of where you can bring reconciliation. Record them around the circles above.

In the end God will fully restore everything, and heaven and earth will be one again. But until that time you have a mission. Jesus called people to repent and believe in the gospel, for the kingdom of heaven is near. It's nearer than you thought. It's not a detached spiritual realm we float into after we die. It's living under His authority as our King right now. With His Spirit you don't have to go across the world to be a missionary (though He might call you to do that). You can begin carrying out the Great Commission right where you are. You're an ambassador of the kingdom of heaven here on earth. Today.

How would you explain the gospel? Write a summary of the gospel story.

3. KINGDOM LIFE

Did you notice in your previous study that the mission Jesus gave His followers sounds a lot like something we saw back in Genesis? Jesus told the disciples to go make more disciples in all nations as His witnesses in Jerusalem, in Judea and Samaria, and to the ends of the earth (see Matt. 28:19; Acts 1:8). In the beginning God told Adam and Eve to be fruitful and multiply, filling the earth with His image and likeness (see Gen. 1:28).

Making disciples is the ministry of reconciliation.

Making disciples is being fruitful and multiplying.

The whole earth is to be filled with the image and likeness of God. When a king rules over a kingdom, His image is spread throughout the land so that everyone knows who has authority. You can still see this practice in modern times. In the United States, for example, you see flags, seals, symbols like the eagle, and even pictures of presidents on our money. During the time of Jesus, tension existed between the cultures of the religious Jews and the Roman Empire. Some leaders tried to force Jesus into saying something controversial.

Read Mark 12:13-17.

What did Jesus say belongs to the earthly government?

What did He imply belongs to the kingdom of God?

What does that distinction look like practically? How can you give God your life today?

The denarius with Caesar's image on it also had a title inscribed on it declaring his authority and divinity. Jesus, the true Son of God, reminded everyone that we should give ourselves to God because we're created in His image. We represent His kingdom.

The Spirit conforms us more and more to the likeness of Jesus as we follow Him in obedience. Jesus commanded us to continue His mission of inviting other people into a right relationship with God. So what does a spiritually fruitful life look like? What should be growing in us and being reproduced in others?

Read Galatians 5:22-23.

Record the fruit of the Spirit on the pieces below and answer the questions.

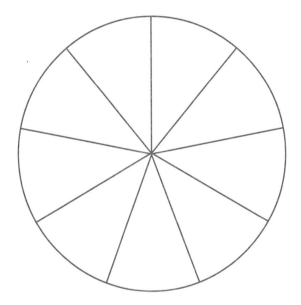

The characteristic that's hardest for me is:

I see God growing me in this area:

Notice that these are described as "fruit of the Spirit" (v. 22), not fruits. Each trait is a piece of the whole. When the Spirit is at work within you, you'll be conformed to the likeness of Christ in all these characteristics. Don't get discouraged if it doesn't happen immediately. Fruit takes time to grow, and there are seasons. But this is what a healthy life looks like.

Let's drill down into one of those areas right now. Though all of those characteristics are part of the same fruit, Jesus focused on one that you might think of as being the root that gives life to the rest of the fruit or maybe the part that surrounds it all:

> I give you a new command: Love one another. Just as I have loved you, you must also love one another. By this all people will know that you are My disciples, if you have love for one another.
> **JOHN 13:34-35**

The context of this command is important. In the verses just before this, Jesus had washed His disciples' feet, even the feet of Judas, who'd already agreed to hand Jesus over to be arrested and crucified. Judas was about to walk out of the room, betraying Jesus—God with us—for a sack of silver coins. Jesus, once again, modeled God's humble love for us by literally getting down on His hands and knees to wash their feet. This was the lowest form of service in that culture. Imagine how filthy feet were in a time when most roads were dirt, most shoes were sandals, and all forms of transportation involved animals that left a mess everywhere. Immediately after these verses even Peter, one of Jesus' closest friends, would deny even knowing Him. Jesus then willingly surrendered to those who hated Him and died sacrificially on the cross so that anyone who believes in Him can be reconciled to God and receive a new, eternal life (see John 3:16).

Read the following passages and beside each Scripture record words or phrases that summarize Christian love.

Matthew 5:43-48

Matthew 22:34-40

1 Corinthians 13:4-7

1 John 3:16-18

1 John 5:3

Whom do you know who's a picture of Jesus' love and can help you grow spiritually? Record as many names as possible.

Don't be afraid to ask that person (or people) questions or advice on understanding and living out the truth in God's Word. Talk to them soon, maybe right after you finish your study.

Who's the hardest person (or people) in your life to love?

How can you show love and forgiveness to them?

Jesus said this countercultural love is the way the world will recognize Christians. If we're known for anything else—and honestly, we've earned a pretty bad reputation for being unloving in many ways—we need to repent, ask for God's forgiveness, and allow the Spirit to grow healthy fruit in our lives. Remember, He wants to give us abundant life (see John 10:10).

When you understand that you're created in the image of God and filled with His Spirit, you know that the greatest need of everyone around you is to enter this life-giving kingdom.

With whom will you share the gospel message of love and forgiveness, leading them to be reconciled with God?

Wrap up by thanking God for His amazing, undeserved love.

God proves His own love for us in that while
we were still sinners, Christ died for us!
ROMANS 5:8

SESSION FOUR

SCARS

START

Welcome everyone. Start by reviewing session 3 before introducing session 4.

Session 3 focused on the kingdom of heaven.

What was most helpful, encouraging, or challenging from your personal reading and reflection in session 3?

Today we'll shift our focus to healing in this life.

What scars do you have, and how did you get them? Briefly share stories.

What, if anything, did you learn from the experience when you were wounded?

Everyone gets hurt. Keep the following question in mind as we watch the next video.

What wounds need healing or have been healed in your life?

WATCH

Use the space below to take notes or sketch ideas as you watch the video for session 4.

SCRIPTURES: Psalm 103:3; Matthew 9:12-13; 2 Corinthians 1:3-5; Leviticus 16:1-22; James 5:16; Isaiah 53:5; Matthew 3:17; John 20:24-29

RESPOND

Use these statements and questions to guide a group discussion.

Jefferson shared a time in his life when he was struggling. The grace he was shown was a turning point in his relationship with God.

Whom has God used to show you grace and unconditional love? How did that person encourage you? How did his or her example help you better understand a relationship with God?

What turning points have you experienced in your relationship with God?

When have you felt that you weren't healing or finding peace?

What stories do you have about times when Jesus healed your wounds?

Read John 20:24-29.

What's most encouraging to you about the way Jesus responded to Thomas? Why is that encouraging?

When have you struggled to believe something about Jesus? How did you overcome your doubt and start believing?

With what questions about Jesus do you still wrestle? How can you give those questions to God, trusting Him even when you can't see the answer?

What else in the video was helpful, encouraging, or challenging for you? Why?

Wrap up with prayer. Encourage everyone to complete the personal reading and reflection on the following pages before your next group session.

MORE FROM THE BOOK: To go even deeper into the topics covered in this session, read chapter 8 in *It's Not What You Think: Why Christianity Is About So Much More than Going to Heaven When You Die* by Jefferson Bethke (Thomas Nelson, 2015).

PERSONAL READING & REFLECTION
1. OUR MANY WOUNDS

You know the drill by now. Let's start with a quick review of what we've covered so far before diving into what's next. In the previous session you saw three major points:

1. You saw what it really means to live as part of God's kingdom, not just in heaven when you die but right now on earth. This gospel message is radically countercultural.

2. As the King with all authority, Jesus gave you a mission. You're an ambassador of His kingdom who's been assigned the ministry of reconciliation, creating pockets of heaven on earth wherever you go.

3. The Spirit conforms you more and more to the likeness of Jesus as you continue His mission of inviting other people to be reconciled to God through His love.

By now you may be thinking this can't apply to you. You may think you're too jacked up or have done too many bad things to be a Christian. Or if you're already a Christian, you may think you have to settle for being on the JV squad, riding the bench as you sit on the sidelines and let the professionals share the gospel and do real ministry. But that's not an option. At least not according to the Great Commission Jesus gave us. You saw in the previous session that even His own disciples didn't get it right all the time and bumbled along in their journey. So you can find comfort in that fact and in these three facts this week:

1. We all have wounds. Some of these are inflicted by our own sin, other times we're injured by others' sin, and we all experience pain and suffering in a broken world.

2. Our God doesn't just know about our suffering; He knows what it feels like to suffer. Although Jesus never sinned, He was tempted and hurt, getting the full human experience.

3. Because Jesus was perfect, His sacrifice was the only one that could reconcile us to God and bring true healing. As we experience His healing, God reveals a new purpose in our pain.

It all starts by recognizing our problem, and God's Word makes it abundantly clear:

All have sinned and fall short of the glory of God.
ROMANS 3:23

In other words, we're all jacked up. We're rebellious. We're selfish. We're sinful.

Every. Single. One of us.

All have sinned.

And falling hurts.

So this session, especially this section, is going to be a little sensitive. Just know that right up front. You're going to be asked to identify your hurt. Your pain. Your wounds. But also know that the whole point of acknowledging your wounds is so that you can experience healing. You don't need to hide your wounds. Hiding a wound—ignoring it and pretending it doesn't exist—only makes things worse. When we don't deal with that sensitive spot, that deep cut, it begins to fester and grow more painful as it swells and becomes infected. Right? This is no time to pretend you've got it all together, hiding behind a religious or moral mask with a big smile painted on it as if everything's fine. Life isn't all sunshine and Skittles®, rainbows and unicorns. That's a fantasy. You need to deal with real life.

Christianity isn't a game of make-believe, and the church isn't full of perfect people. Look at Jesus' words:

The healthy don't need a doctor, but the sick do. I have not come to call the righteous, but sinners to repentance.
LUKE 5:31-32

The first thing you have to do is admit that you have a sin problem. Identify specific sins in your life, even from today (for example, attitudes, actions, desires, addictions, words).

What wounds have your sins caused in your life? Be specific.

What wounds have your sins caused in other people's lives? Be specific here too about ways you may have hurt others.

That first type of wound is self-inflicted. Your sin has consequences. It's yet another ripple effect. You experience the painful consequences of your own sin. Not only did sin break your relationship with God, but it also continues to hurt your day-to-day life.

You also saw that your sin can hurt others. This leads to the second type of wound you experience—wounds inflicted on you by other people.

How have you been hurt by other people?

Read Romans 8:18-23.

Describe natural disasters or other ways the world is broken.

How have you been hurt by the brokenness of the world?

We've already seen that God created the world in perfect harmony and said it was all good. But we broke everything. Even the natural world suffers now from our sin. There are sickness and death, emotional and mental disorders, natural disasters and freak accidents. Everything from the core of the earth to the DNA in our bodies has been wrecked by sin.

Think of it like this. Roads are intended to work a certain way. It's not unloving to tell people to do certain things and not to go a certain way. That's how things work best for the sake of everyone's good. It's loving to teach people the right way to do things and to warn them of any danger.

Imagine you're driving down the interstate, and you decide you want to turn across the lanes or drive in the opposite direction. Not only do you put yourself in danger, but everyone around you is at risk of being hurt also. You may seem to get away with your behavior for a while, but you're going to get hurt or even die.

Now imagine that you cause a wreck. This can happen in two ways: either you crash into another car, or you hit a physical structure like a wall or a bridge. Either way, shrapnel is ripped off your vehicle or from the structure and scattered across the roadway. Other cars that come later are now in danger of running into your wreck or the damaged roadway, causing them to wreck.

Of course, you could just as easily be the one who in that moment is doing nothing wrong. You can be driving along innocently when you hit a massive crack that blows out your tire. Maybe you get smacked by a reckless driver from any direction imaginable. Of maybe you're simply not able to stop in time when you come up on someone else's collision that happened long before you got there.

Sin is like the chain reaction in a multicar pileup on the highway. It affects you, others, and even the way things are supposed to work. Everything starts breaking down. Sometimes you make bad choices. Sometimes other people make bad choices. Other times pain isn't directly related to anybody's action; bad things just happen.

> **What wounds do you still have—sensitive or painful areas that you're afraid to let anyone, maybe even Jesus, get near?**

> **What's keeping you from trusting Jesus to heal those wounds?**

We all have wounds. Some of these are inflicted by our own sin, other times we're injured by others' sin, and we all experience pain and suffering in a broken world. But there's a light at the end of the dark tunnel. We can have hope because God has a remedy.

> **We'll look at the remedy next, but to fully appreciate the good news of healing and life that Jesus offers, let the reality of sin and brokenness sink in and allow yourself to feel your wounds.**

2. WHEN GOD WAS A MAN

God loved the world in this way: He gave His One and Only Son, so
that everyone who believes in Him will not perish but have eternal life.
JOHN 3:16

We're broken. The world is broken. But we don't have to perish. Our story doesn't have to end in disaster. All hope isn't lost.

Two thousand years ago God injected the remedy to our sin into the stream of human history.

Our God doesn't just know about our suffering; He knows what it feels like to suffer. Jesus was tempted and taunted, beaten and betrayed, hungry and humiliated. He lived in this broken world, and He even died. Jesus had the full human experience, more than most of us have experienced, yet He never sinned.

We can't dismiss this too quickly, thinking, *Of course He didn't sin. He was God.* But He was also human, remember? Completely. One hundred percent human. Flesh and bone.

The fact that God became a man and walked the same earth that you're sitting on right now as you read this is pretty incredible. The same air filled Jesus' lungs as He breathed. His eyes looked up to see the same sky. He slept. He wept. He got tired. He got hurt.

But we saw before that when Jesus was tempted to give in to do things His own way instead of trusting God's good will for His life, He resisted that human urge. He quoted the Word of God. He didn't give up when life was hard (see Matt. 4:1-11).

Jesus. Never. Sinned.

This fact is massively important for three reasons that completely reorient the way we relate to God.

1. Jesus was the perfect man.

Just as through one man's disobedience the many
were made sinners, so also through the one man's
obedience the many will be made righteous.
ROMANS 5:19

Sin entered the world through the first man, Adam, and righteousness and reconciliation with God are made possible through the perfect man, Jesus (see Rom. 5:12-21). When Adam and Eve sinned, every person born after that inherited a broken, sinful nature.

What patterns of sin do you see in your own family (for example, temper, addiction, bad relationships)?

How have you seen a sinful inheritance in your life? In other words, are your tendencies in certain sins more like your family than you may like to admit?

What wounds have been caused by sin in your family?

What tendencies do you hope you won't pass on if you have children or if you'll have children someday?

How can Jesus break that cycle of sin in your life?

We've all inherited a mess. But we can't blame the generations behind us. We've all made our own messes too.

Jesus knows this. Though He never sinned, He knows from experience what it's like to grow up in a family. Before He was born, His earthly father considered divorcing His mother. Jesus was the oldest child of Mary, a teenage girl who got pregnant before she was married. Though this was miraculous in nature, it's not hard to imagine the gossipy whispers and judgmental looks about "that girl." He grew up in a poor family. We know this because He was born in a barn and laid in a feeding trough and because Mary's offering at the temple was two pigeons, the offering for someone who couldn't afford a lamb. Jesus' family wasn't perfect either. When Jesus was a little kid, Mary and Joseph left Him behind during a family trip and lost Him for three days. Even His own siblings thought He'd gone crazy and was taking this whole spirituality thing too far (see Lev. 12:8; Matt. 1:18-25; Mark 3:20-35; Luke 1:26-38; 2:21-24,41-50). This isn't to say those things are sinful but simply to emphasize that Jesus understands difficult family dynamics.

How does knowing that Jesus experienced family life and had to grow up just like everybody else make you feel?

2. Jesus was the perfect priest.

We've seen that after sin entered the world, breaking humanity's relationship with God, the way God came down to relate to His people—Remember the steps from session 2?—was through the tabernacle and the temple. This holy space—Remember the overlapping circles from session 3?—was where heaven and earth overlapped, so to speak. And the whole thing was dependent on an incredibly detailed sacrificial system carried out by priests.

But if Jesus was already the perfect man, wasn't that enough to hit the reset button on everything? As always, God didn't take any shortcuts. He was completely satisfying every detail in His redemptive purpose. The whole story had been pointing to Jesus all along.

> Since we have a great high priest who has passed through the heavens—Jesus the Son of God—let us hold fast to the confession. For we do not have a high priest who is unable to sympathize with our weaknesses, but One who has been tested in every way as we are, yet without sin. Therefore let us approach the throne of grace with boldness, so that we may receive mercy and find grace to help us at the proper time.
>
> **HEBREWS 4:14-16**

Though these verses may sound abstract, circle the very practical conclusions presented in the first and last sentences.

In what ways is this passage encouraging, especially in the midst of suffering?

What does the fact that Jesus faithfully endured and never gave in to sin tell you about temptation, trials, and suffering?

3. Jesus was the perfect sacrifice.

From the beginning of His earthly ministry to the prophetic vision of future realities, the same images are used for Jesus as the ultimate sacrifice:

> The next day John saw Jesus coming toward him and said,
> "Here is the Lamb of God, who takes away the sin of the world!"
> **JOHN 1:29**

Over and over in Revelation, a book full of prophetic imagery, Jesus is pictured as a lamb, even a slaughtered, sacrificial lamb (see Rev. 5:6; 7:17; 14:10; 15:3; 19:6-9; 22:1-3).

When Jesus died on the cross as the unblemished lamb and perfect sacrifice, everything changed. In His death Jesus fulfilled everything He came to do in His life. The sacrificial system was no longer necessary. The priesthood was no longer necessary. God had warned Adam and Eve that sin would end in death. The first Adam failed. Jesus, the perfect Adam, was faithful. Sin did end in death. Jesus' death buried our sin forever.

Read Isaiah 53. Then use the space below to record words or phrases that capture your attention and stir feelings of sorrow for sin, gratitude for Jesus' ultimate sacrifice, or awe and worship.

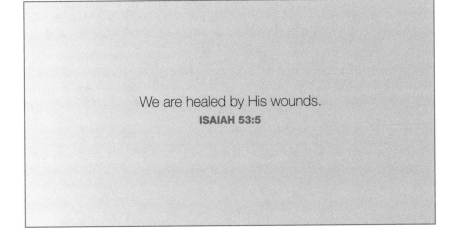

We are healed by His wounds.
ISAIAH 53:5

3. PURPOSE IN OUR PAIN

It is finished!

JOHN 19:30

Jesus spoke these words before He died on the cross. But that was two thousand years ago. Why, then, didn't the story end there? Or with His resurrection three days later? Or with His ascension from earth to heaven 40 days later? Why did God add the step of sending the Holy Spirit? Why does human history continue to race along like a runaway train?

Why does a good God allow suffering to continue moment after moment, day after day, year after year, generation after generation? What's He waiting for?

If you've ever wondered about any of those things, you're not the first. In one of his letters, which is now part of the New Testament in your Bible, Peter, one of Jesus' closest friends, answered this question. People were already (and understandably) eager for Jesus to return and complete His ministry of reconciliation. They wanted God to make everything right again, bring it all back into order, and bestow the peace of His presence forever.

But think about it. If God had ended the story before now, you wouldn't be here. It's easy to get impatient once you're part of the in crowd, so to speak. It's kind of like when you were a kid playing musical chairs, and you wanted the music to end as long as you had a seat, but who cares about anyone else, right?

Look at what Peter had to say about it:

> The Lord does not delay His promise, as some
> understand delay, but is patient with you, not wanting
> any to perish but all to come to repentance.

2 PETER 3:9

Because Jesus was perfect, His sacrifice was the only one that could reconcile us to God and bring true healing. As we experience His healing, God reveals a new purpose in our pain. Our wounds become scars. Our scars become stories.

And God loves the world so much that Jesus didn't just die for you or me but for everyone who will believe in Him. People need to hear your story. People need to hear His story.

The story.

When and about what have you been impatient with God?

What's something you didn't understand at the time but later saw how God used it for good in your life or in someone else's life?

> We know that all things work together for the good of those
> who love God: those who are called according to His purpose.
> **ROMANS 8:28**

Notice that verse doesn't say everything is good. As Christians, we can't pretend that because God is good, everything is good. To do that can seriously hurt other people by belittling their pain. Pain is real. But God is more real, and He can use even bad or painful things to accomplish good things for the good of those who love Him and "are called according to His purpose."

Yes, we're blessed, and we have hope and joy in Christ, but we don't have to be phony about it. Nobody likes a fake, and one is easy to spot. It can do a lot of damage to always walk around saying, "I'm blessed, Brother," and "PTL, Sister" (that's "Praise the Lord" for my text-illiterate friends reading this) without ever admitting that life is hard and that you get hurt. Most people who act this way have either never cared enough about anything to be hurt or, more likely, are hiding from pain.

It's amazing that we can even hide behind seemingly spiritual facades. But that's not new either. Jesus warned hypocites about hiding behind religious and moral appearances, calling them whitewashed tombs full of rotten bones (check out Matt. 23:27-28)!

How do you try to hide your wounds?

How is hiding unhealthy for you? How is it unhelpful for others?

God is calling you, like Adam and Eve, out of hiding. You can't cover your own shame. Only the grace of God and the sacrifice of Jesus can clothe you in His righteousness. It's human nature to try and pass the blame. Adam and Eve tried after the first sin. But God didn't except their excuses then, and He won't accept yours today. You're responsible for your own sin (and for how you react to sin and brokenness around you).

What excuses do you make for sin?

At this point you might be wondering how you can experience healing. Practically speaking, what can you do? What does it look like to come out of hiding and stop making excuses?

Confess your sins to God and to other people in your church family. Be honest about being happy, being sad, or needing prayer. Pray and keep praying until God works according to His timing. Do all these things so that other people can be saved from their sins too (see Jas. 5:13-20).

Jesus' suffering enabled Him to help us:

> Since He Himself was tested and has suffered,
> He is able to help those who are tested.
> **HEBREWS 2:18**

This is true of the wounds and scars we bear too. The hurt and healing we experience tell the gospel story to others, allowing us to relate to them in a deeply meaningful way so that they can ultimately understand that their true need is spiritual; they need Jesus and the cleansing of their sins:

> Praise the God and Father of our Lord Jesus Christ, the Father
> of mercies and the God of all comfort. He comforts us in all our
> affliction, so that we may be able to comfort those who are in any
> kind of affliction, through the comfort we ourselves receive from
> God. For as the sufferings of Christ overflow to us, so through
> Christ our comfort also overflows. If we are afflicted, it is for your
> comfort and salvation. If we are comforted, it is for your comfort,
> which is experienced in your endurance of the same sufferings
> that we suffer. And our hope for you is firm, because we know that
> as you share in the sufferings, so you will share in the comfort.
> **2 CORINTHIANS 1:3-7**

If you're reading this, you're conscious, your heart and mind are working, blood is still pumping through your veins, and breath is still filling your lungs. That means there's still time to repent right now, believe in Jesus, and be healed. The same is true for the people around you.

You have wounds. Jesus has healing. You have scars. People need the story.

Use the rest of this page to record some ways Jesus has healed areas of hurt, guilt, and shame in your life.

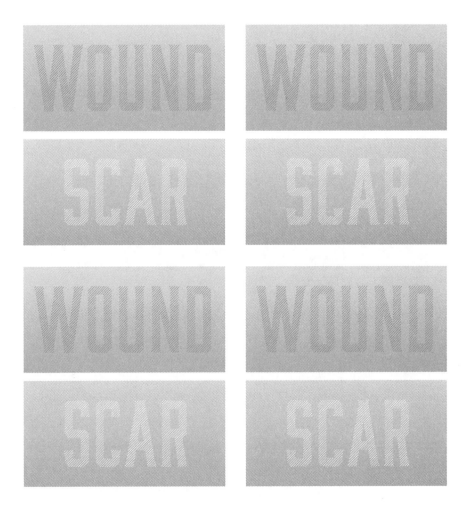

Practice telling stories of ways the good news of Jesus has changed your life, even though you're still not perfect.

SESSION FIVE

IDENTITY

START

Welcome everyone. Start by reviewing session 4 before introducing session 5.

Session 4 focused on how Jesus turns painful wounds into scars that tell a story.

What was most helpful, encouraging, or challenging from your personal reading and reflection in session 4?

Today we'll shift our focus from what our scars say about Jesus to what He says about us.

What does your name mean, and why were you given that name?

What nicknames have you had, and how did you get them?

Do you like your name or your nicknames? Why or why not? Briefly share names and answers.

The way our identity is defined is more important than we may realize. Keep the following question in mind as we watch the next video.

Who or what defines your identity?

WATCH

Use the space below to take notes or sketch ideas as you watch the video for session 5.

SCRIPTURES: John 11:25; 1 Corinthians 15; Matthew 3:13-17; 1 Samuel 16:13; Mark 1:9-15; Luke 15:11-24; 1 Kings 19

RESPOND

Use these statements and questions to guide a group discussion.

When have you had a hard time discerning God's voice? Why did you want to hear from Him?

When have you clearly experienced God's presence? How did you know it was God?

Read 1 Kings 19:9-18.

In what ways did God reassure Elijah that He was with him?

When have you wanted God to speak or act in a powerful way, but He didn't do things the way you expected?

Read Matthew 3:13-17.

Why is it significant that God said He was pleased with Jesus before He began doing miracles and ministry?

What does this expression of approval reveal about God? About your relationship with Him? About your identity?

Honestly, who or what is currently determining your actions and defining your identity?

If anyone has been baptized, what significance did that act have in your life? Why were you baptized? If you haven't yet been baptized, what keeps you from being baptized?

What else in the video was helpful, encouraging, or challenging for you? Why?

Wrap up with prayer. Encourage everyone to complete the personal reading and reflection on the following pages before your next group session.

MORE FROM THE BOOK: To go even deeper into the topics covered in this session, read chapters 4 and 6 in *It's Not What You Think: Why Christianity Is About So Much More than Going to Heaven When You Die* by Jefferson Bethke (Thomas Nelson, 2015).

PERSONAL READING & REFLECTION
1. WHEN GOD WHISPERS

As is our routine, let's start with a quick review of what we recently covered before diving into what's next. In the previous session you saw these three major points:

1. We all have wounds. Some of these are inflicted by our own sin, other times we're injured by others' sin, and we all experience pain and suffering in a broken world.

2. Our God doesn't just know about our suffering; He knows what it feels like to suffer. Jesus was tempted and hurt, getting the full human experience, although He never sinned.

3. Because Jesus was perfect, His sacrifice was the only one that could reconcile us to God and bring true healing. As we experience His healing, God reveals a new purpose in our pain. Our wounds become scars that tell a story of healing and salvation.

As we seek to move forward in healing and freedom, we're likely to wrestle with the following questions.

1. What happens when you really want to see or hear God, but He isn't showing up as you expected? Does that mean something's wrong with your relationship with God?

2. How does our behavior relate to our identity? Is there anything we can do to make God love us more or less?

3. What's a step in the right direction when we seek to live as part of God's kingdom? How do we begin living out our identities as children of God?

It may seem funny to say so, but it's helpful to remember that the people in the Bible were real people. Yes, we're reading their stories thousands of years later, and yes, they experienced God in amazing and sometimes supernatural ways, but they were ordinary people. The extraordinary, miraculous events we read about were written down exactly because they're so extraordinary and miraculous. It wasn't the everyday experience of every person who ever loved God to see and hear Him.

That wasn't even the everyday experience for people like Abraham, Moses, the prophets, or even Jesus' disciples as they began the church. Of course, the disciples saw God every day when they were with Jesus, but they didn't realize He was God at the time, and surely some days were pretty normal. After all, Jesus was constantly explaining things or reminding them about what He'd just said or done. Remember the time He fed thousands of people with a kid's sack lunch, and then they hopped into a boat and started to freak out? "Oh, man! We forgot to bring something to eat. Now what are we going to do?" (see Mark 8:16-21).

People described in the Bible were real people with real thoughts, emotions, and concerns. Like them, we have moments when we don't know what to believe about God and our relationship with Him. So to be encouraged, let's look at two guys in biblical history who didn't quite know what to do when life wasn't meeting their expectations, and neither was God. Then we'll look at two women who have a great lesson for us as well.

Read 1 Kings 19:1-18.

When have you felt alone, especially as a Christian?

When have doing the right thing and trusting God seemed to make life harder instead of easier?

We've all heard stories or testimonies about someone who lived a crazy life and then met Jesus, and everything went happily ever after. But for most of us, living by faith doesn't make things look better. Sometimes it seems to make things worse.

In this passage Elijah sure doesn't look like one of the most famous prophets in history. He doesn't look like one of the great heroes of faith. He was falling asleep depressed and overwhelmed to the point of wishing he were dead. He was running scared from a woman he really ticked off. He was ignoring God's miraculous provision and worried about being killed. And finally, he was whining about being all alone when God informed him that there were actually seven thousand people who'd remained faithful. Seven thousand nameless people who didn't have their stories written down in Scripture, but God saw them.

Remember how important context is when trying to understand the story of Scripture? In the two chapters before this story Elijah experienced God's power by changing the weather, was miraculously fed in several different ways, called down fire from heaven in a my-God-can-beat-up-your-god contest against hundreds of self-mutilating pagans, and raised a little boy back to life from the dead for a kind widow. Wow. It's no wonder he was at the end of his rope. But he'd also grown accustomed to seeing God work in big, impressive ways.

When have you wanted God to show up in a big way, but instead you got a whisper?

We've already seen a few times during this study that actually being with Jesus didn't make things easier to understand or believe. Look at one of the most famous stories when a disciple, wrestling with human emotions and doubts, needed Jesus to show up.

Read John 20:24-29.

Imagine what Thomas must have been thinking and feeling before Jesus showed up. The other disciples said they'd all seen Jesus. If it was true, why didn't he get to experience it? Why would they make something like that up? Didn't Jesus care about him as much as He cared about the others? Were they messing with him in some cruel way as he grieved the death of someone he was close to? What on earth was going on? What should he believe?

What's most encouraging to you about the way Jesus responded to Thomas?

Why is that encouraging?

When have you struggled to believe something about Jesus? Or with what questions about Jesus do you still wrestle?

How has Jesus met you in your doubt and helped you believe?

This disciple got stuck with the unfortunate nickname of Doubting Thomas. Two thousand years later we still use that phrase for skeptics. But one of the greatest parts of this story, one that's often overlooked, is how Thomas responded after Jesus showed Thomas His scars. (Scars really do tell great stories that can bring people to faith!)

Thomas responded to Him, "My Lord and my God!"
JOHN 20:28

How can you worship Jesus personally even when you don't fully understand God?

Finally, let's look at a story about two sisters.

Read Luke 10:38-42.

Summarize what each sister was doing. Draw a star next to the one Jesus commended for making the right decision.

Mary:

Martha:

It's easy, especially in this generation, to think you always have to do something meaningful for your life to matter, and by meaningful I mean some epic adventure or sacrificial service. But sometimes all you need to do is sit at the feet of Jesus and quietly listen as He whispers.

Spend time right now being quiet and still. Use Jesus' prayer for all His disciples in John 17 to listen to Him. Use the prayer Jesus taught His disciples in Matthew 6:9-13 to guide anything you say to Him in response.

2. EARNING YOUR IDENTITY

Chances are your first job was something that paid close to minimum wage. Your wage is what you earn from your work. It's the fruit of your labor, so to speak. No matter whether or not somebody likes you, there's a legal obligation to pay workers their wages. The employer owes the employee payment for the work done.

Look at what the Bible says about the payment you've earned each time you've chosen to do things your own way instead of trusting your Creator and King:

> The wages of sin is death, but the gift of God
> is eternal life in Christ Jesus our Lord.
> **ROMANS 6:23**

The bare minimum you're owed is death. These words have echoed throughout the pages of history since the first man and woman sinned. God warned them that the payment for sin was death, but they didn't believe God's instruction was best for them. In the context of this verse in Romans, there's a metaphor explaining that when you sin, you're choosing to work for sin. You're a slave, and sin is your master. That master is cruel and abusive and punishing, but the payment is fair. The payment you're legally owed is death.

That's a sobering reality. You deserve death. You've earned it. We all have. (But saying "we" doesn't help too much in softening that harsh fact, does it?) It's true. That's the bad news.

But the good news—the gospel—is that God is a good Master. King of kings. He freely offers the gift of eternal life through faith in Christ Jesus our Lord. *(Lord* isn't just a word referring to God but literally means *Master.)* This free gift is called *grace.*

It's easy to start thinking that somehow God owes us, and we deserve something from Him. But notice Romans 6:23 doesn't say we work for Him now. It says He gave us a gift.

Why? Because He loves you.

Honestly, when have you felt as if God owed you something, especially for your good behavior?

If you think about it, believing God will give you good things if you're good and bad things if you're bad is believing you can manipulate God. That's not a relationship. That's a vending machine or a cosmic robot at best. If you push all the right buttons in the right order, then the things you want will pop out. It's all about learning the right codes.

That's not Christianity. That's a pagan idea. That's what those guys Elijah battled on Mount Carmel believed when they hopped around, shouting and cutting themselves and hoping their god would send fire down from heaven. It never came.

How often do you beat yourself up for bad behavior? Put an *X* on the scale below.

How often do you pat yourself on the back for good behavior? Put an *O* on the scale below.

1	2	3	4	5	6	7	8	9	10
Never									Always

Do you believe God is more or less pleased with you, based on your behavior?

Yes   No

Do you believe God is more or less likely to give you what you want, based on your behavior?

Yes   No

Jesus gave us something infinitely better than religious hoops to jump through to earn God's favor. He introduced the world to a personal relationship with a loving Father. At the time it completely broke the system. People couldn't handle the idea of a guy calling God His dad. Jesus was saying that anybody could join the family, no matter their race, gender, or background.

One of the best stories in Scripture to illustrate just how scandalous God's love truly is can be found in Luke 15. In this chapter Jesus tells three parables: the parable of the lost sheep, the parable of the lost coin, and the parable of the lost son. Tim Keller writes in his book *The Prodigal God* that this parable could better be understood as the parable of the two lost sons.[1] This is the story we're going to look at now. It's truly mind-blowing.

Read Luke 15:11-32.

Did you see it? This has to be one of the most unexpected plot twists ever, but we might not even catch it at first. Jesus just flipped the script on everybody.

This story is amazing, and here's why. Jesus was telling this parable to the Pharisees. The religious elite. The ones who thought they deserved God's blessings. They were the older son. Yet the older son, who stayed home, was just as lost as the younger son, who indulged every earthly desire to party and have what seemed like a good time. The older son hated the idea of the father being gracious toward the younger son, who had been so wildly immoral. The older son felt that the father owed him more than the younger son because he'd always kept the rules.

This story is usually told for the sake of those who identify with the younger son. He knew he'd been selfish and stupid. He could easily see the painful situation he'd gotten himself into by choosing a life apart from his father.

It's easy to spot the sins of people caught up in self-indulgence, partying, and casual relationships. It's a lot harder to recognize the sins of people who are caught up in self-righteousness, legalism, and moral comparison.

Both sons took their father for granted. Both sons just wanted the blessings and benefits of their father without enjoying his presence and a relationship with him. Both sons were lost. But only the younger son confessed and repented, coming back to the father (even though he thought he could pay him back by working for a servant's wages). The father was full of passion as he humbled himself by running, something no dignified man would do in that culture, to bear-hug the son who'd come home. And then they threw a real party.

Circle your most recent condition on the scale below.

Record an X to indicate the most extreme point in your life.

1	2	3	4	5	6	7	8	9	10

Ashamed: rock bottom   **Arrogant: looking down**
in the pigpen   **from a moral pedestal**

Which son do you most often resemble—the younger, immoral son or the older, judgmental son? Explain your answer.

In what are you seeking your identity?

Experience   Pleasure   Wealth   Ability   Morality   Other:

If you've a hard time knowing where your sense of identity comes from, ask yourself what you couldn't be happy without.

What makes you angriest?   What makes you happiest?

The older son got angry because his whole system of ideals, the way life worked, and his sense of identity and value came crashing down. When his father didn't show him special treatment for his behavior, he didn't know what to do and was left standing outside the party. But the gracious father gave both sons the choice to enjoy his generous love.

This story isn't just about them; it's about you too. Look at what God's Word says about your identity and relationship with Him:

> When the time came to completion, God sent His Son, born of a woman, born under the law, to redeem those under the law, so that we might receive adoption as sons. And because you are sons, God has sent the Spirit of His Son into our hearts, crying, "Abba, Father!" So you are no longer a slave but a son, and if a son, then an heir through God.
> **GALATIANS 4:4-7**

What do these verses say about your identity? Circle key words.

What do they say about your ability to work for God and to earn His approval?

Spend a few minutes thanking God for adopting you into His family, welcoming you with open arms, and giving you the free gift of an inheritance in His kingdom.

1. Timothy Keller, *The Prodigal God* (New York: Dutton, 2008), 17.

3. BACK TO THE FUTURE

Everybody loves a good story about time travel, right?

Throughout this study we've been looking at what the Bible says about how we can live each day knowing the end of the story. Well, technically, the story goes on forever, but what I mean by the end of the story is the time when God ultimately restores all things, bringing everything back into alignment with His purposes. But until that day comes, *we're* that point of overlap.

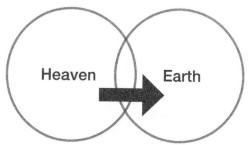

As Christians, we live out our future reality in the present. We live on earth as citizens and heirs of the kingdom of heaven. We leave the old in the past and live in our future identity:

> You took off your former way of life, the old self that is corrupted by deceitful desires; you are being renewed in the spirit of your minds; you put on the new self, the one created according to God's likeness in righteousness and purity of the truth.
>
> **EPHESIANS 4:22-24**

We get a glimpse of this transformation from old to new in baptism. The gospel is visibly demonstrated in baptism, which testifies to our identity in Christ and the family of God.

> We were buried with Him by baptism into death, in order that, just as Christ was raised from the dead by the glory of the Father, so we too may walk in a new way of life.
>
> **ROMANS 6:4**

It's like traveling through time.

Baptism is a before-and-after picture.

Past, present, and future are all tied up in that moment.

Have you been baptized?　　Yes　　No

If so, describe when and where it was and who was there.

Why was it a significant experience for you?

Read Romans 6:1-11.

Summarize the meaning of *baptism,* as described in these verses.

All this talk about death might sound morbid at first. But it's actually a beautiful and hopeful picture. There's a tension between sorrow over sin and celebration of salvation. It's not just a picture of death. It's a picture of rebirth and resurrection.

In baptism you identify with the Son of God. You have joined His family and will enjoy life as His coheir. You get to hear the same voice spoken over you that Jesus heard:

> After Jesus was baptized, He went up immediately from the water. The heavens suddenly opened for Him, and He saw the Spirit of God descending like a dove and coming down on Him. And there came a voice from heaven:
>
> This is My beloved Son.
> I take delight in Him!
> **MATTHEW 3:16-17**

How much would it mean to you to know without a doubt that God is pleased with you? Think about your answer and mark a point on the scale.

1	2	3	4	5	6	7	8	9	10
Nothing									Everything

Don't miss this. This is huge. The voice of God our Father declared His pleasure with Jesus before He'd performed one miracle, taught one thing, or died on the cross.

God's delight in Jesus was based solely on His identity. His love was based on their relationship as Father and Son.

The exact same thing is true for you too.

God's delight in you is based solely on your identity. His love is based on your relationship as Father and child of God.

Once again, we're not just talking about an abstract picture. The Bible gives practical instructions for how to live out your resurrected identity as a child of God and a coheir with Christ.

Read Colossians 3:1-17.

On the left write the negative qualities to put to death.
On the right write the positive qualities to put on.

OLD SELF   NEW SELF

Pause here to pray about these two lists. Ask for God's grace in helping you put to death your old self and to do everything in the name of Jesus.

Finally, read the following sections of Romans 8 as a prayerful act of worship, letting God speak to you through His Word.

If you're willing, read the verses aloud, especially 35-39, so that you can literally hear the Word of your Heavenly Father assuring you of His unconditional love and your freedom as His child.

No condemnation now exists for those in Christ Jesus, because the Spirit's law of life in Christ Jesus has set you free from the law of sin and of death. What the law could not do since it was limited by the flesh, God did. He condemned sin in the flesh by sending His own Son in flesh like ours under sin's domain, and as a sin offering, in order that the law's requirement would be accomplished in us who do not walk according to the flesh but according to the Spirit.

ROMANS 8:1-4

All those led by God's Spirit are God's sons. For you did not receive a spirit of slavery to fall back into fear, but you received the Spirit of adoption, by whom we cry out, "Abba, Father!" The Spirit Himself testifies together with our spirit that we are God's children, and if children, also heirs—heirs of God and coheirs with Christ—seeing that we suffer with Him so that we may also be glorified with Him.

ROMANS 8:14-17

Who can separate us from the love of Christ?
Can affliction or anguish or persecution
or famine or nakedness or danger or sword?
As it is written:
Because of You we are being put to death all day long;
we are counted as sheep to be slaughtered.
No, in all these things we are more than victorious
through Him who loved us.
For I am persuaded that not even death or life, angels or rulers,
things present or things to come, hostile powers,
height or depth, or any other created thing
will have the power to separate us
from the love of God that is in Christ Jesus our Lord!

ROMANS 8:35-39

TABLE

START

Welcome everyone. Start by reviewing session 5 before introducing session 6.

Session 5 focused on your identity as a child of God.

What was most helpful, encouraging, or challenging from your personal reading and reflection in session 5?

Today we'll wrap everything up in what may seem to be a surprising topic.

What's the best meal you've ever had, and what made it so great?

The table is a place where we gather every day, and it points to a bigger and better story. Keep the following question in mind as we watch the final video.

How does my life tell the story of a God who wants us to enjoy abundant life now, not just eternal life in heaven?

WATCH

Use the space below to take notes or sketch ideas as you watch the video for session 6.

SCRIPTURES: Luke 24:13-32; Luke 22:1-38; Luke 5:30-31; Revelation 19:6-9

RESPOND

Use these statements and questions to guide a group discussion.

Does your life tell the story of God wanting us to enjoy abundant life now, not just eternal life in heaven? If so, how? If not, how can it?

Read Luke 22:14-20.

The Passover meal was originally celebrated to commemorate God's miraculous deliverance of the Israelites from slavery, establishing them as a unique people who were free and set apart from the rest of the world, with God as their King.

How did Jesus give this meal new meaning? How does the original meaning help you understand what Jesus was doing?

How does your church celebrate communion? How can you remember the great significance of this time instead of letting it become a religious routine?

Read Luke 24:13-35.

How does this story reveal that all of Scripture, even the Old Testament, is a story about Jesus?

How does this story reveal that being taught about Jesus is a good starting point but not the same as truly knowing Jesus?

What else in the video was helpful, encouraging, or challenging for you? Why?

Jefferson wanted to show that being a Christian is more than just going to heaven. What's your greatest takeaway from this study?

Wrap up with prayer. Encourage everyone to complete the personal reading and reflection on the following pages to conclude this study.

Plan a meal to celebrate what God is doing in your lives as a group and invite new people to join the group before you begin your next study.

PERSONAL READING & REFLECTION
1. EAT, DRINK, REMEMBER

You made it! Well, almost. You've made it this far in the final session, and if you're still engaged, I think you're going to finish this study. I really pray that this has been an eye-opening and life-changing experience for you. Hopefully, this will be just one step, maybe even the first step, in a long journey as you follow Jesus, bringing little pockets of heaven to earth everywhere you go.

One last time let's start with a quick review of what was covered last time before diving into what's next. In the previous session you saw these three major points:

1. Sometimes you really want to see or hear God, but He doesn't show up as you expected. At times God whispers, and we need to learn to listen carefully.

2. Your behavior is an overflow of your identity. You can't earn your relationship with your Heavenly Father. There's nothing you can do to make Him love you more or less.

3. Baptism is a picture of what Jesus has done in the past and of the future reality of resurrection. In Jesus your old self is dead, buried, and resurrected; you were made new.

This final session will wrap everything up by looking at three more truths:

1. In Jesus' final day before His crucifixion, He had one last meal with His disciples. Why?

2. Everything we do and don't do in this life matters. Your work and your rest are acts of worship pointing toward the kingdom of heaven.

3. God created us to enjoy life in His presence now and forever. This is amazing!

There are a few extra pages at the end of session 6 that will help you think through everything you've learned. Thanks for coming on this journey with me!

MORE FROM THE BOOK: To go even deeper into the topics covered in this Bible study, finish reading *It's Not What You Think: Why Christianity Is About So Much More than Going to Heaven When You Die* by Jefferson Bethke (Thomas Nelson, 2015). For more about Sabbath and the table specifically, read chapters 5 and 9.

After a short ministry of about three years with His disciples, just before Jesus was betrayed, arrested, tried, beaten, mocked, and executed, He knew what was about to happen, and He did something amazing.

If it were me, and I knew what was about to happen and that these guys were about to begin the greatest work and most important mission the world has ever known—a movement that literally changed the course of human history—I'd have been having a cram session to make sure everybody knew their role. We'd have gone over key teaching, strategy, whatever.

You know what it's like before a big trip or a big game. You're going over all the last-minute details, checking and double-checking to make sure you've thought of everything, everybody involved is at the right place at the right time, and you have plans if anything unexpected happens.

But Jesus didn't do that. Yes, He gathered His closest friends. And yes, He provided some instruction but not in a way that anybody expected. (Which basically summed up the entire life of Jesus, right? Nobody expected Jesus to be, say, or do almost any of the things He was, said, and did.) Jesus, the Son of God, just hours before He was betrayed by a close companion and murdered for crimes He didn't commit, sat down and had a meal.

Read Luke 22:7-23.

How would you describe Jesus' tone and the atmosphere of this scene?

What does it say to you about Jesus that He shared this time with Judas, knowing the plan for betrayal?

A few of the things happening here are pretty amazing and worth pointing out. First, it's pretty incredible that Jesus told Peter and John they'd find a guy in town carrying water and to follow him to a house and ask the owner of that house where the room was that Jesus could use. No names were given. No address was given. Just find a guy, go to that house, and ask for the room.

Can you imagine Peter and John walking into the city and looking for some random dude carrying a jug? After they finally found the guy, they tailed him like spies in a chase scene back to a house before asking the owner where the room was for their group to use for

Passover. And the guy gave them a room! That's a small miracle in itself. The fact that carrying water was almost always a chore done by women not only made the guy a little easier to identify but also made Jesus' awareness of the extraordinary detail even more miraculous.

All that's pretty cool, but the meal itself is what's most significant. Jesus and the disciples were observing the Passover, so it's worth checking out the original story of the Passover to understand why Jesus chose to observe this meal in His final hours. Below are some key verses, but if you have time, you may want to read all of Exodus 12 for the bigger story.

Read Exodus 12:2.

The observance of Passover would remind God's people of a new beginning in their lives. The calendar would literally start over to begin with this significant event.

Why did our calendar reset with a starting point of just over two thousand years ago? What do B.C. and A.D. refer to in our calendar today?

Whether or not people choose to worship Jesus, He literally changed history and is the life around which all history revolves. Everything is measured in relation to Him.

Read Exodus 12:5-7.

What was to be killed in observance of Passover?

Notice the communal nature of what was happening. There was a collective responsibility for killing the Passover lamb. The blood of the lamb was then to be spread on the wooden posts of each doorway.

Read Exodus 12:12-13.

What did judgment (death) or salvation depend on?

Read Exodus 12:24-28.

Why is the observance called Passover?

How does this account point to Jesus' death on the cross?

This is amazing, yet it's easy for us to miss this symbolism today. Notice that even though God's salvation of His people ultimately pointed to Jesus, Jesus perfectly kept the commands of God through His final hours. While observing the Passover, He provided clarity as to its ultimate meaning with His disciples that night. Look at the radical nature of the two statements Jesus made to redefine the significance of the Passover:

> He took bread, gave thanks, broke it, gave it to them, and said, "This is My body, which is given for you. Do this in remembrance of Me." In the same way He also took the cup after supper and said, "This cup is the new covenant established by My blood; it is shed for you."
> **LUKE 22:19-20**

God had commanded His people to observe this meal in remembrance of the salvation He gave them from bondage. When Jesus said to remember Him, He was saying that He was God, He was the one providing true salvation, and by His blood alone the judgment of death would pass over someone. This was the most radical thing a person could possibly say. It would have been absolute blasphemy and insanity. Unless it was true.

Within hours Jesus was betrayed. He was killed as the perfect Lamb of God. His body was broken, and His blood would be poured out, staining the wooden crossbeams. All of history would be reset and measured by His life. Now through faith in Christ, anyone could enter the community of God's people.

Today we live according to the new covenant that Jesus proclaimed.

Read Jeremiah 31:31-34.

Thank God for putting this new law in your heart, freeing you from sin, judgment, and death. Because of Jesus, you can know God.

2. BE STILL

There's an anonymous artist who's most famous for his social commentary through graffiti. It's not really fair to call it graffiti, because if you're not familiar with Banksy, you probably imagine vandalism by a kid with a can of spray paint tagging a bridge, street sign, or train car with crude or colorful lettering. Banksy's art mysteriously pops up overnight with a clever perspective or thoughtful commentary. One image, called "Mobile Lovers," appeared on a door in April 2014 in Bristol, England, depicts a man and a woman embracing each other and appearing to look into each other's eyes. The twist comes when you realize that both are looking past each other and checking the glowing cell phones they're holding up behind each other's head.

It seems that as a culture, many, if not most, of us have lost the art of unplugging and simply being in the moment. We're addicted to knowing what's going on somewhere else and to letting people know what we're doing. We're always doing something, even if it's simply eating a meal or enjoying a cup of coffee. Don't check now, but chances are you'll see a picture of somebody's meal or latte art if you scroll through social media today.

Now social media is a great thing. We probably have more technology and information at our fingertips than we had when we put the first man into outer space. (Yet we get frustrated if a video on Netflix or YouTube buffers for a second while we stream it.) It's amazing and wonderful that we can stay in touch with and get to know people all over the world in ways we never could before, not even 5 to 10 years ago.

I think something really interesting is happening, although we've missed the point a bit. Built into us, by God's design, is the desire for connection and relationship. Social contacts, especially meals, are intended to be shared communal experiences. Let's go back to Genesis to look at three things God said "in the beginning" (1:1).

First, do you remember the pattern in the creation process when God pronounced each day that it was good? There's something fascinating about the fact that even before sin entered the world, there was something God said wasn't good.

Read Genesis 2:15-25.

What was the first thing God said wasn't good (see v. 18)?

What two words are used to describe woman in relation to man?

There's a beautiful picture of Adam breaking into song when he saw Eve for the first time. In fact, in verse 23 the text in your Bible is probably indented to set it apart because it's poetry. Adam got all romantic when he saw the first woman. Then we see the world's first marriage, because Eve is called his wife in the final two verses following Adam's song (see vv. 24-25).

Obviously, this doesn't mean God thinks it's bad to have some alone time. And it doesn't mean we should never be alone. Woman and man complement each other. This isn't talking about saying nice things to each other, although we should—and Adam did woo Eve with the first love song—but it means marriage is a unique relationship. We'll see by the end of this session that it's even more distinctive than we may think. It points to an even bigger and better story. The meaning here, though, is that, like God, who exists as Father, Son, and Holy Spirit, and everything else in creation that has a counterpart, human beings were created to be in relationship. We're made for community.

What distracts you from genuine, meaningful relationships?

How can you be intentional about developing meaningful relationships?

Who are your closest relationships?

Do they encourage you in your relationship with God?

Notice that Eve is also called Adam's helper (see v. 18). Before God said it isn't good for man to be alone, God had given him work to do. Work isn't a result of sin and a broken world, although it got harder after the fall (see Gen. 3:17-19). God originally created man and woman to joyfully participate in satisfying, meaningful work. As those uniquely created in His image and likeness, they were assigned authority over all of God's creation. They named the animals and cared for the garden.

Think back to the session 5 when we read Colossians 3:1-17. We saw that in Christ we're being restored to God's design in the garden. That passage reminds us that the image of God is being renewed, we're united in one body (symbolically, not physically), we should sing together in praise of God's goodness, and our work should be worshipful and good.

What work do you enjoy most?

How can you honor God in everything you do (even in what you may not enjoy so much)?

Finally, look at the last day of creation. God does something else amazing that we often overlook or take for granted. Next to our relationship with Him and with one another, it's one of His greatest gifts.

Read Genesis 2:1-3.

What did God do on the seventh day?

A day of rest is so much more than going to church on Sunday. I don't know exactly what it means for God to rest, but in doing so, He blessed a day of rest, making it holy before any established religion ever existed. Sabbath is more than a religious observance. It's part of God's rhythm for life.

Not only is rest good for us, but it's also an act of worship. It doesn't have to be a strict, legalistic observance. The point is to stop and recognize that God created and provides everything we need, so we can trust Him to take care of us. If God can rest, we can rest.

It's bad for us to always feel we have to do something. In a sense we're saying we don't trust that we'll be taken care of, have what we need, or be satisfied unless we always work.

Weirdly enough, worshipful rest is something we have to be intentional about. It may take a little planning or a lot of self-control. Apparently, rest goes against our nature so much that God has to command it. In the Ten Commandments only Sabbath and idolatry get more than a single verse explaining the importance of those commands (see Ex. 20:8-11).

Read Hebrews 4:1-11.

How do you carve out time for rest and worship?

What refreshes you?

The Sabbath, a time of worshipful rest, is yet another picture pointing to a bigger and better story. In these verses God revealed that ultimately, a time of rest is coming in which only those who've responded to the gospel of Jesus will receive the blessing of holy, worshipful rest forever.

Remember the story of Mary and Martha in session 5? Martha thought she could best honor Jesus by rushing around busily working for Him. But Jesus said Mary's resting at His feet and listening to His words were the best things to do in that moment. Work is a gift from God, part of His design for our lives, but it has to be balanced with intentional, focused rest. Both work and rest are acts of worship as we follow God's example and command:

> Be still, and know that I am God.
>   I will be exalted among the nations,
>   I will be exalted in the earth!
> **PSALM 46:10, ESV**

Take time to "be still" and rest in God's presence. Commit to intentionally and regularly set apart time to worship God and trust that in His goodness you have everything you need.

3. A FORETASTE OF FOREVER

You might remember Jesus' words from session 4, when we looked at how Jesus can heal our wounds, but now let's go back and look at the whole story to get the bigger context.

Read Luke 5:27-32.

Matthew was a tax collector. You know how much people hate paying taxes now, but in Jesus' day tax collectors were known to be of questionable character, often skimming a little off the top to keep for themselves. In addition, think about the tension between the culture of the Jewish religion and the Roman Empire. Those feelings of hatred would get cranked up another few notches when a Jew collected taxes, kept some for himself, and gave the rest to the Roman Empire. This is scum-of-the-earth, two-faced, backstabbing, traitor kind of stuff.

Yet Jesus not only ate with this guy and his friends, but He also called Matthew to leave everything behind from his old way of life and follow Him into a bigger and better story. The religious establishment, which liked to pretend they had it all together, didn't like Jesus' tactics. Jesus was clear that in His kingdom, life is about knowing we need His love and forgiveness so that we can live each day with gratitude. Then we start bringing those little pockets of heaven on earth to everyone in our circle of influence. People's lives are transformed, wounds are healed, and sinners are reconciled to God.

Think of ways you can use a meal to share the love of Jesus.

Go ahead and plan at least one meal when you'll invite someone to join you. Maybe even plan a regular time and day of the week to meet someone and build the relationship in a way that encourages you both to grow spiritually.

WHEN   WHERE   WHO

That's what Christianity is all about. It's always been about experiencing God's kingdom "on earth as it is in heaven" (Matt. 6:10). It's about relationship. It's about growth. It's about life change. It's so much more than just going to heaven when you die.

Nevertheless, we'll experience eternal life. We look forward to the day when heaven and earth are brought back into alignment. It's just that we don't wait for it. We start living that future reality now. We get tastes of it here, like appetizers or samples before the great feast.

When that day finally comes, it'll look something like this:

> I heard something like the voice of a vast multitude, like the sound of cascading waters, and like the rumbling of loud thunder, saying:
>
>> Hallelujah, because our Lord God, the Almighty,
>> has begun to reign!
>> Let us be glad, rejoice, and give Him glory,
>> because the marriage of the Lamb has come,
>> and His wife has prepared herself.
>> She was given fine linen to wear, bright and pure.
>
> For the fine linen represents the righteous acts of the saints.
> **REVELATION 19:6-8**

You may not think of yourself as a saint, but you are. The word *saints* means *holy ones.* When you take off the old self and put on the new self, you're being clothed in the righteousness of Christ. He makes you holy. His love for you cleanses you from sin and impurity, and your life becomes fine linen adorning His bride.

The Bible is clear that marriage is and always has been a picture of Jesus and His bride— the church. We're the bride of Christ. You and everyone who believes in Jesus for the forgiveness of sin and a new life are the church:

> For this reason a man will leave
> his father and mother
> and be joined to his wife,
> and the two will become one flesh.

> This mystery is profound, but I am talking about Christ and the church.
> **EPHESIANS 5:31-32**

Are you seeing this? God's Word says since God created and blessed Adam and Eve, He had in mind a picture of Jesus, you, me, and every saint in the church.

From Genesis to Revelation the story has been about God's reconciling people to Himself.

God will ultimately restore all things, bringing heaven and earth back into alignment:

> I saw a new heaven and a new earth, for the first heaven and the first earth had passed away, and the sea no longer existed. I also saw the Holy City, new Jerusalem, coming down out of heaven from God, prepared like a bride adorned for her husband.
>
> Then I heard a loud voice from the throne:
> Look! God's dwelling is with humanity,
> and He will live with them.
> They will be His people,
> and God Himself will be with them
> and be their God.
> He will wipe away every tear from their eyes.
> Death will no longer exist;
> grief, crying, and pain will exist no longer,
> because the previous things have passed away.
>
> Then the One seated on the throne said, "Look! I am making everything new." He also said, "Write, because these words are faithful and true." And He said to me, "It is done! I am the Alpha and the Omega, the Beginning and the End. I will give water as a gift to the thirsty from the spring of life. The victor will inherit these things, and I will be his God, and he will be My son."
>
> **REVELATION 21:1-7**

Do you see how it all comes around full circle and ties together in the end?

The story is complete. But it goes on forever.
God dwells with His people. Forever.
The kingdom is established. Forever.
Every wound is healed. Forever.
We become children of God. Forever.
We eat, drink, and live. Forever.

I don't know if you get emotional at weddings, but weddings typically pull out all the stops. They're a big deal. Because they happen only once in a lifetime, the bride and the groom look their very best, everyone they love is invited, and the biggest celebration imaginable is thrown in honor of the happy couple. They pledge their faithfulness to each other for the rest of their lives.

This is the picture of eternal life.

This is heaven crashing into earth in the most spectacular way imaginable.

Heaven isn't a boring place in the clouds with chubby babies flying around strumming harps. It's the perfect union of God's realm and ours. It's the marriage of Christ and the church. It's the story God has been telling since "In the beginning …" (Gen. 1:1).

It's the picture God painted when presenting the first woman to the first man. And what they broke, He made new. It's the consumation of all things.

Recall the curse of sin at the beginning of the story, when God sent Adam and Eve out of the garden so that in their sin they wouldn't eat from the tree of life, dooming them to remain apart from His presence forever (see Gen. 3:24). In the future God will reverse this curse and invite us to enjoy the fruit of the tree of life. Look at the end of the story:

> He showed me the river of living water, sparkling like crystal, flowing from the throne of God and of the Lamb down the middle of the broad street of the city. The tree of life was on both sides of the river, bearing 12 kinds of fruit, producing its fruit every month. The leaves of the tree are for healing the nations, and there will no longer be any curse.
>
> **REVELATION 22:1-3**

Before continuing, pause to reflect on the hope and affection stirred in your heart to know that God has pursued you and has a plan to be with you forever.

At the beginning of each group session there was a question to keep in mind as you watched the videos. Each question is listed below. Answer these questions aloud in a group discussion and/or write your thoughts here for personal reflection.

1. How does the way I view the Bible affect my life?

2. If the story in the Bible about a relationship with God is true, how will you respond?

3. Who or what is in the position of authority over your life?

4. What wounds need healing or have been healed in your life?

5. Who or what defines your identity?

6. How does my life tell the story of a God who wants us to enjoy abundant life now, not just eternal life in heaven?

THE MODEL PRAYER

You should pray like this:

Our Father in heaven,

Your name be honored as holy.

Your kingdom come.

Your will be done on earth as it is in heaven.

Give us today our daily bread.

And forgive us our debts,

as we also have forgiven our debtors.

And do not bring us into temptation,

but deliver us from the evil one.

[For Yours is the kingdom and the power

and the glory forever. Amen.]

MATTHEW 6:9-13

	I USED TO THINK ...	NOW I BELIEVE ...
About the gospel		
About the Bible		
About God		
About Jesus		
About the Spirit		
About the Christian life		
About heaven		
About God's kingdom		
About myself		
About other people		